HIDDEN TREASURE HOUSES

HIDDEN TREASURE HOUSES

JAMES MILLER

1804906840

MACMILLAN

First published 2006 by Macmillan
an imprint of Pan Macmillan Ltd
Pan Macmillan, 20 New Wharf Road, London N1 9RR
Basingstoke and Oxford
Associated companies throughout the world
www.panmacmillan.com

ISBN-13: 978-1-4050-9127-5
ISBN-10: 1-4050-9127-4

1 3 5 7 9 8 6 4 2

A CIP catalogue record for this book is available from
the British Library.

Typeset by Perfect Bound Ltd
Colour Reproduction by Aylesbury Studios Ltd. Bromley Kent
Printed by Bath Press

For my mother, Jean,
who endured my endless juvenile questioning

Contents

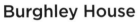

Preface

During the last two years, somehow spliced between my work for Sotheby's, I have had the good fortune to be involved with Channel Five's series *Hidden Treasure Houses*. This has meant summer months filming in some of the most beautiful and interesting houses in Britain, followed by winter ones putting together the programmes. They have been a delight to make and whilst writing this book I have been mentally revisiting them all. As with the series, a chapter has been devoted to each house so that its special characteristics can be explored, for, as you will discover, no house is like any other.

I cannot remember a time when I was not fascinated by the country houses which gently populate the British landscape. They are so much part of the fabric of the land that you might almost take them for granted, except that each is so original. I am often teased by friends who cannot believe I still get pleasure driving up yet another long gravel driveway towards an unknown house . . . but I do. It has always been so. I can well remember the journeys, taken when I was a young boy, from north Oxfordshire to my grandparents in the Cotswolds. After a few miles we encountered the florid gates of Middleton Park topped with urns and large stone rats as supporters. Then, after passing the remnants of Second World War airfields, we would drop down into the Cherwell valley and here on one side was Rousham, embowered in William Kent's arcadian landscape, whilst across fields stood a large eye-catcher directing you towards Thomas Archer's Aynhoe. On another hill stood Aston, a curious house built directly into the parish church, whilst across the main Oxford to Banbury road was a majestic avenue of Wellingtonias both heralding and hiding Barton Abbey. Nearing the village of Enstone, the leafy domain of Tew Park could be glimpsed to the north, whilst the great pile that is Heythrop came and went from sight as the road ran up and down. To my boyhood eye these were entrancing sights: a series of great buildings settled in their landscapes. To my boyhood mind they presented an endless list of questions: when were they built; who built them; who lived there; and what had happened to them over the years? My delight in these buildings and that flow of questions has never diminished. These houses are an endless variation on a theme; variations created through the aspiration and taste of generations of owners who have responded individually to the challenge of their creation and development. Exploring these variations is what made making the programmes so fascinating. I hope you will enjoy reading about them here.

I know I have been lucky. I have worked at Sotheby's for more than thirty years, which has given me the opportunity to visit a large number of country estates. My old diaries are full of odd references to houses, many of which I had not heard of until I visited. These have subsequently become part of my 'map' of Britain. I remember first visiting Brodsworth in Yorkshire, an unlikely Italian palazzo built to the west of Doncaster by the Thellusen family in the nineteenth century. You could just catch sight of it from the A1 but otherwise it was a realm apart. The main gates were kept locked and to reach the house I had to make my way up a narrow track near the old gardens. This led eventually to the main front, its stone discoloured by pollution, the windows firmly shuttered and the great metal rings that were supposed to support its columns lying like hula hoops at their bases. In contrast to the building's forlorn appearance was its chatelaine, Mrs Grant Dalton, who, despite confessing she would really prefer to live in a 'plain Georgian box', had valiantly kept the house going. There she sat, among the naked white marble statues acquired by her husband's ancestors, championing the right of the house to continue – and to continue not in isolation but as part of the community. It was typical that during the miners' strikes she insisted that what produce there was in the walled garden should be handed out to the strikers' families who lived nearby. Brodsworth showed me how vulnerable the future of such houses could be and how their loss would deeply affect the cultural, economic and social basis of innumerable small communities. Nowadays Brodsworth is much better known; its future secured by English Heritage.

By a curious twist of fate Sotheby's asked me to run the Country House Sales Department, dealing with the sales of their contents. It meant my love for these buildings and their collections was often harnessed to the end of a particular chapter in their history. I quickly learned that nothing in them has arrived by its own volition and that every object is part of a vast jigsaw puzzle, a reflection of the activities of generations of owners. It is the interconnection between works of art, the family and the buildings that brings the individual qualities of each house to life. Sometimes it took time to piece it all together. At Benacre in Suffolk I came across a small panel painting lurking in a drawer full of defunct electrical equipment. It appeared to be Italian and possibly dates from the early years of the Renaissance. Research proved these initial thoughts were right; in fact it was by the great early master Cimabue. But what was that doing there, surrounded by equine paintings and Georgian furniture? Whilst I had come across a reference in an early inventory to a small picture of a Madonna and Child, proving it had been there since the late nineteenth century, it was not until I went to look at the family tombs that I found that one of the family had died in Florence in the 1830s. It transpired she was a cousin of the earliest English collector of early Renaissance works, and so everything finally fell into place. This painting, emerging from obscurity, not only increased our knowledge of thirteenth-century Italian art but also our understanding of this particular family and English collecting in general. As you will discover, this dialogue between the history of a house, its owners and the works of art found there is one of the absorbing things about these buildings.

In choosing the houses explored in the series I have shamelessly selected ones that I particularly love and have exploited friendships made with their owners over the years. I first arrived at Dalmeny in the late 1970s to help rearrange the collection following a sale for the Earls of Rosebery at Mentmore, and I feel as if I have been part of the furniture there ever since! Stanway I got to know in my twenties and have since witnessed the brilliant transformation of its landscape. I still clearly remember my first visit to Berkeley Castle, enthralled by its ancient splendour but curious as to how the whole collection had come together and who had been responsible for the rebuilding of the castle in the early twentieth century. It was another decade until papers emerged in the old estate office that helped to unravel this mystery, adding yet another layer to the building's fascinating history.

Like many people I first encountered Scampston looking across the park from the road. I subsequently gave way to my curiosity and, when an opportunity arose, asked if I could visit. In those days the service wing was being rebuilt for Charles and Caroline Legard, whilst Charles's mother lived in the main block. There was talk then of them staying in the side wing but who could resist the challenge of restoring the house when the time came? Now the house and gardens have been brilliantly refurbished and brought to life – like all the houses in this series, there is much to celebrate.

The celebrations at Deene took place at the millennium when Edmund and Marion Brudenell erected an obelisk topped with a tea pot – a deliciously idiosyncratic gesture that aptly sums up the seriousness that has underpinned their work, as well as the wit with which it has been carried out. It will also add to the architectural confusion of this splendid house where there are already endless contradictions. The portrait of the original owner turns out to have been painted a good 150 years after his death and Lady Cardigan's bed (so appropriate in its setting) has only recently returned, having been banished from the house for nearly a century. At Sherborne Castle it seems that generation after generation have celebrated their good fortune at living here by altering and improving this astonishing building. Now it is John and Jo Wingfield-Digby who are making their mark before passing on the baton to the next generation. At Burghley, the baton-passing is currently taking place as Simon and Victoria Leatham relinquish their roles. If ever a house was fortunate it is Burghley. During the last twenty years the Leathams have been uncovering its history and bringing this great Elizabethan house back to life. Queen Victoria's visit may have been beset with problems in the 1840s, but no such misfortunes would occur now.

Arundel and Holker make an interesting contrast; both ducal houses rebuilt in the nineteenth century, but whilst one was the principal family seat the other was a place of quiet retirement. In both cases the houses almost defeated the families, but both have flourished again in this generation. Defeat also stared Penshurst in the face in the late eighteenth century, and likewise at Goodwood a few years later, but there is a strong resilient streak to the Sidney and Lennox families that gave them the courage to stay and prosper. In fact in all these houses there has been an ebb and flow. As Victoria Leatham says, the economic cycle can look like a fever chart in a hospital — one moment you are up and the next right down. Wild bursts of extravagance are followed by periods of deep retrenchment. At Burghley, such financial constraints mean that even the floorboards could not be laid in the state rooms for some fifty years following the 5th Earl's death. He may have left pictures by the score and tapestries by the dozen, but he also left huge debts.

Not only have these houses survived in the hands of descendants of their original owners, but also the present owners are actively involved in continuing to improve them and their collections. Edmund Brudenell, for instance, is still trying to locate books taken from Deene by Cromwellian soldiers; the Legards have enabled family portraits by Gainsborough to find their way back to Scampston; and Henry Cavendish's microscope is now in the library at Holker thanks to his descendant Hugh. These collections continue to grow and evolve, each in its own distinct way, and that simple fact is what contributes to the fascination of these houses. Most of the families can trace their fortunes back to the sixteenth century. Almost all were affected by the Civil War but recovered and prospered in the late seventeenth century, and in the next century properties and collections were enhanced – often as a result of the Grand Tour. This overall history is very consistent but the individual responses to the opportunities thrown up are mind-bogglingly diverse. Even rather close family connections between houses can have surprisingly little effect. There is hardly anything at Deene, Goodwood and Berkeley to link them despite the fact the Duchess of Richmond was a Brudenell and her daughter, Louisa, married Lord Berkeley. Each family history, as expressed in their houses and collections, is a truly beguiling and wholly individual story.

Arundel Castle, Sussex

The seat of the Dukes of Norfolk

L ooking from the east across marshy ground where tall reeds obscure the course of the River Arun, the great building of Arundel Castle fills the far escarpment. The skyline bristles with crenelated towers and turreted chimneys, and the massive walls of dressed stone and split flint rear up against the sides of the small valley. The castle was originally built to defend this gap in the natural defences of the South Downs, and it still dominates the landscape. The building is a sharp reminder of the might of the Norman barons who built it and testimony to the tenacity of the FitzAlan-Howards, Dukes of Norfolk, the direct descendants of William de Albini, 1st Earl of Arundel, who lived here in the early twelfth century.

Take a closer look, though, and a more complex picture emerges. Are the walls really Norman and do the great towers truly belong to the reign of Henry III? There seems to be a crispness and regularity to the building that suggests that all is not so straightforward. Is Arundel really a medieval castle? Yes and no. Like many great houses in Britain, its history is much more complicated. The castle is certainly on the site of the fortified building erected on the order of William the Conqueror soon after the battle of Hastings and William de Albini's ancient keep still dominates the internal courtyard. Yet much of the building you see across the Arun valley is a spectacular rebuild, dating from the nineteenth century. In effect this is a new castle: built on those ancient foundations and redolent with the family's illustrious history. It was re-created to provide a seat consonant with the importance of its owner, the Premier Duke of England, hereditary Earl Marshal, and secular head of the Roman Catholic Church in Britain.

This building is the embodiment of the family's position and influence. Its form, style and even its layout reflect this; the Baronial Hall is vast, dwarfing everything and everybody; the Castle Chapel is a disciplined Gothic beauty, evocative of England's Catholic past; and the suite of rooms along the south front are in effect state apartments. Behind them is the Long Corridor of the picture gallery, where family portraits of the FitzAlan-Howards, Dukes of Norfolk, hang chronologically, illuminating their enduring and eventful history. Here are displayed the family's great possessions accumulated over the centuries and brought here at different times. Despite or perhaps because of the complexity of its development, Arundel is one of the most fascinating houses in England.

It is also one of the friendliest, with nothing remotely stuffy to discourage the visitor. Typically, on my arrival I was met not just by Richard the butler but by the bicycles and balls of the duke and duchess's five children. The current Duke

and Duchess, Eddie and Georgina, live in a family wing on the east side. Before their arrival in the later 1980s this wing had been largely abandoned. They decided that these rooms, built as family apartments for the 15th Duke in 1875, should be returned to their former use. Now, as elsewhere in the castle, there is here a clever synthesis between the strong Victorian architecture and the daily needs of a young and growing family. These rooms continue to evolve. When I was last there the old Billiard Room had been reinstated on the first floor, following the nineteenth-century layout. This has now given way to a relaxed Sitting Room, with deep comfy sofas surrounding a roaring fire set beneath a Victorian stone canopy, littered with fabric samples and swatches (evidence of further work in progress). The duchess, who was once employed by the decorators Colefax & Fowler, is steadily bringing the whole building back to life. This, I discovered, is the latest chapter in a story that stretches back over the last 160 years.

In 1842 Bernard Edward, 12th Duke of Norfolk, died. He had inherited the Dukedom from a distant kinsman twenty-two years earlier but had chosen not to live at Arundel. During his tenure, the castle was a desolate sight. Sir Robert Peel, before he became prime minister, noted: 'The whole scene was a melancholy one. The whole castle is deserted, and the present Duke dislikes it as a residence. He has removed the books from the Library, and I should think the carpets and furniture from the other rooms. There is not a single fire except the kitchens.' This state of affairs was not to last. His son Henry, 13th Duke, and his enterprising wife, Lady Charlotte Leveson-Gower, decided to make Arundel their principal country home and embarked on a process of improvement and restoration that would last until the end of the century. Initially, refurbishment of the principal rooms was put in hand, stimulated by an impending royal visit. The duke was Master of the Horse to Queen Victoria, and the duchess was a favourite lady-in-waiting. Just two years after they inherited, the queen informed them that she would like to visit the castle and a date was set for 1846, two years hence.

The Norfolks summoned the most fashionable decorator of the day, G. J. Morant, whose skills had already been employed by the duchess's father, the Duke of Sutherland, at Stafford (now Lancaster) House off The Mall in London. According to an article in the *Illustrated London News*, Morant 'refitted [Arundel] in a style of gorgeous magnificence for the proper reception by England's premier Duke of his Sovereign and her Royal Consort'. For instance the Great Drawing Room was 'hung with paper of gold and green, of the richest design . . . The curtains and chair coverings are of splendid crimson and gold silk damask'. Internally the scene was transformed from desolation to splendour, yet externally it was difficult to disguise the hotch-potch nature of the architecture. Queen Victoria was clearly of the same opinion. In her diary she favourably compared the layout to 'ours' at Windsor but said of the exterior 'the castle has not been restored in good style . . . and Saxon and Gothic architecture are mixed'. The duke and his son made attempts to remedy this, but with the latter's premature death in 1860

Opposite: The Chapel of Our Lady designed by Charles Alban Buckler and built between 1894 and 1898.

the work ceased and was not revived until the middle of the next decade. This hiatus had some advantages. By the mid 1870s the necessary funds had been garnered for a more coherent approach; the new duke proved to be one of the most sensitive and committed of patrons and his chosen architect was a perfect match. Arundel today is the result of that happy confluence.

The patron was Henry, 15th Duke of Norfolk (1847–1917); his architect the Catholic convert, antiquarian and goth, Charles Alban Buckler. Theirs was a brilliant partnership; Buckler took great delight in working for a client who played an active role whilst the duke admired Buckler's seriousness and commitment. They shared an intense admiration for the Gothic architecture of the thirteenth century – robust walls, soaring arches, and an infinite variety of carefully placed ornaments – coupled with a respect for recent innovations in domestic services. Arundel is a building with a Baronial Hall that boasts not only a hammer-beamed roof derived from that at Westminster Hall, and tall lancet windows based on Henry III's palace at Winchester, but also electric light and an ingenious system of underfloor heating. Modern conveniences rarely found in such scholarly medieval settings!

The brilliance and inventiveness of the architecture is perhaps best caught on the Grand Staircase. Nothing prepares you for the shock of its scale, intricacy and inventive use of ornamental details. It is approached at a tangent down the understated picture gallery, with its plain stone walls, simple natural carving and a modicum of light. Turning into the stairwell, the architectural temperature suddenly rises. With no historical precedent to fall back on, Buckler created a soaring secular equivalent of a cathedral transept. High above is a vaulted roof striped with contrasting white chalk and creamy Painswick stone. It is supported by shafts of polished marble and lit by three huge lancet windows of patterned glass, their borders filled with the Norfolk livery colours of red, white and gold. The stairs rise majestically around this space, the handrail of dark polished Derbyshire fossil contrasting with the richly carved stone balustrade of pierced quatrefoils. Above, the upper section is treated as a four-side clerestory with Gothic arcades supported on coloured marble shafts. From here the ribs of the vaults take off, rising up until held in place by three ceiling bosses, carved with the Annunciation and the infant Christ, his arms outstretched in blessing. This Catholic symbolism is intertwined with that of the family, notably in the statues of St Henry and St Flora, the patron saints of the duke and duchess. The most spectacular sculptural decorations are the large heraldic beasts that squat on their haunches at the top of each newel post. In turn a horse, a stag, a wyvern and three lions proudly hold in their hooves, claws and paws shields painted with the principal Norfolk quarterings. You can sense the tension of the muscles under the stone as their outstretched limbs bear these arms, and their tails seem to swish behind them. The quality of this work is outstanding. Each detail was carefully considered by Buckler, scrutinized by his ducal patron and entrusted to the builders Rattee & Kett of Cambridge.

The style and ornament of the castle speak of more than a nineteenth-century penchant for things medieval. They are a conscious evocation of the family's history and enduring Catholic faith. The restored and rebuilt Arundel was in a sense a monument to the Dukes of Norfolk whose ancestors lie buried in the FitzAlan Chapel which forms part of the parish church. Richard FitzAlan, 4th Earl of Arundel, built this as a collegiate church in the late fourteenth century and in its chancel are a series of magnificent late-medieval family tombs. In the centre, before the altar, lies the founder's son Thomas, 5th Earl of Arundel, and his wife Beatrice, daughter of John I of Portugal. The 5th Earl and his royal Countess lie under Gothic canopies, wearing coronets and robes. Their heads rest on pillows that are being adjusted by small angelic figures whilst heraldic dogs lie at their feet. The countess's hair is held in an elaborately jewelled cage and partly

The Grand Staircase showing the carved heraldic beasts on newel posts.

covered by a hitched veil – the height of fashion in the early fifteenth century. The alabaster has been masterfully carved, suggesting it was worked in the royal workshop at Westminster. A Gothic ironwork palisade protects the tombs and, although the wooden staves have rotted over the years, its candleholders are intact and still in use.

Surrounding the central tombs are further medieval monuments to successive members of this powerful and illustrious family: military commanders in the Hundred Year Wars, leading political figures during the Wars of the Roses and patrons of the arts. These attributes came together in the person of Henry, 12th Earl of Arundel (d.1580), who was present at the siege of Boulogne in 1544, acted as Lord High Constable at the coronation of Edward VI and was patron of the composer Thomas Tallis. It was he, a devoted Catholic, who in the mael-strom of the Reformation saved the FitzAlan chapel from destruction. In 1544 he bought the building and separated the chancel from the nave to form a private chapel, where the family have been buried ever since.

The 12th Earl of Arundel held a series of offices under Queen Mary and Queen Elizabeth I before retiring from public life in 1564 to devote his later years to his estates, rebuilding large parts of the castle to create a Tudor mansion within its walls. He had no male heir as his only son had died in 1556. On Henry's death the estates would pass to his only grandson, Philip, offspring of his younger daughter Mary and her husband Thomas Howard, 4th Duke of Norfolk. It therefore looked as if the inheritance of the FitzAlans, Earls of Arundel, would be subsumed by those of another of the richest and most powerful families in England, the Howards, Dukes of Norfolk. However, in the decades following the Reformation, life for such great Catholic families seldom ran so smoothly.

Opposite: The FitzAlan Chapel, built by the 4th Earl of Arundel in 1380, showing part of the tomb of the 5th Earl and his wife, Beatrice of Portugal surrounded by its ironwork palisade.

The Howards, who like the FitzAlans had remained steadfast in the old faith, had risen rapidly during the previous 200 years, amassing vast estates in East Anglia (the largest in England). Sir John Howard, one of Richard III's most active sup-porters, was created Duke of Norfolk and Earl Marshall in 1483, but when he was killed alongside his king at the battle of Bosworth Field his lands were confiscated and his son attainted. There followed a century of political switch-backing. Sir John's son was re-created Duke of Norfolk following his defeat of James V of Scotland in 1513 at Flodden Field, but his grandson, the 3rd Duke, narrowly escaped execution at the end of Henry VIII's reign – the fate that would befall both his own son and grandson. The latter, Thomas Howard, 4th Duke of Norfolk (son-in-law of Henry, 12th Earl Arundel), was implicated in the Ridolfi plot to replace Elizabeth I with her cousin, the Catholic Mary, Queen of Scots. This cost him not only his life but also the family titles and all the Howard lands. And so when his son, plain Philip Howard, grandson of the last Earl of Arundel, inherited in 1580, the castle and the FitzAlan lands were his sole possession. And matters did not end there.

Philip Howard was arrested in 1585 for trying to leave the country without the queen's permission, was tried for treason, attainted and condemned to death. He was incarcerated in the Tower, where he lingered for a decade before dying of dysentery. All that remained of the shattered inheritances of the FitzAlans and Howards hung by a single thread, Philip's infant son Thomas Howard. Thomas spent his childhood in a remote cottage in Essex as Arundel, so recently rebuilt by his grandfather, had been confiscated by the Crown. Though never himself to be created Duke of Norfolk, he spent his life rebuilding the family's position and fortune. Under the Stuarts his maternal family's possessions, including Arundel, were restored to him and thus the FitzAlan inheritance took the place of the Howards. Arundel Castle would eventually be seen as the ancestral seat of the family who later took the joint surname FitzAlan-Howard.

Whilst Thomas, Lord Arundel, would never live at the castle, it is his paintings and works of art that today immeasurably enrich the collection. Among them are a series of portraits by Sir Anthony Van Dyck. Lord Arundel appears in two of these, both double portraits, one that celebrates his success at restoring the family name and one that looks to the future. In the first, painted in 1635, he is shown with his wife, Lady Alatheia Talbot, whom he married in 1606. She was the daughter of Lord Shrewsbury and it was her landed fortune in South Yorkshire, including the town of Sheffield and her father's prodigy house Worksop Manor, which did much to redress Lord Arundel's financial position. Van Dyck shows her dressed in

peeress's robes adorned with sensational jewels – black diamonds and pearls set in a distinctly old-fashioned style, perhaps an allusion to her family's antiquity. Lord Arundel is dressed in peer's robes to reflect the titles of Earl of Arundel and Surrey that had been restored to him by James I in 1604. Beneath he wears armour and in his hand he holds his baton, clear references to the restoration of the office of Earl Marshall in 1621. Lord Arundel's passion for works of art (which led to his being known as the Collector Earl) is attested to in the background with a white marble bust and a bronze head, *The Arundel Homer*. His collection of classical statuary, the first in England, was assembled in a specially designed gallery at Arundel House. The majority of his pieces are now in the Ashmolean Museum at Oxford, save for the group of altar bases that are displayed in the lower Staircase Hall at the castle. The foreground of the painting is taken up by a globe, turned to show the island of Madagascar in reference to Lord Arundel's plan to colonize the island on behalf of Charles I. This was one of his few schemes not to be realized, which was probably much to the relief of his wife who had been alarmed by reports that the island was overrun with fleas.

Opposite: *The Madagascar portrait of Thomas Howard, 14th Earl of Arundel (1585–1646) and his wife Lady Alatheia Talbot by Sir Anthony Van Dyck.*

Above left: *Thomas Howard, 14th Earl of Arundel (1585–1646), with his grandson young Tom (Thomas Howard), later 5th Duke of Norfolk (1627–1677) by Sir Anthony Van Dyck.*

King Charles I by Sir Anthony Van Dyck.

The second portrait, of Thomas and his grandson (also Thomas), seems to look to the future, perhaps with hopes for the restoration of the dukedom. It is one of Van Dyck's greatest and most sensitive achievements. Lord Arundel stands erect, dressed as Earl Marshall and carrying his baton, his left hand resting on the shoulder of his young relative. The boy, resplendent in a shimmering red doublet enlivened with a double string of pearls, looks out as if pondering his destiny. That future would encompass the Civil War, exile in Italy and Lord Arundel's death there in 1646, but it would also lead to the full restoration of the family's honours. All that his grandfather strove for would finally be achieved in 1660, when Charles II created Thomas the 5th Duke of Norfolk, the title held by his successors ever since.

It is appropriate then that two of the best seventeenth-century works of art in the castle should celebrate Charles I, as it was Arundel's allegiance to the Stuart dynasty that brought about the revival in his family's fortunes. The first is the half-length portrait of the king, another work by Van Dyck, which hangs at the end of the Great Hall. It says much for the artist's power that the painting can hold your attention across such a vast space. You are aware of the royal presence as soon as you enter the far door; the king looks out with a quiet confidence that recalls a contemporary description: 'he would not let fall his dignity – tho' he was far from pride, yet he was careful in his Majesty, and would be approacht with respect and reverence'. The portrait was painted in the later 1630s, by which time Van Dyck was very familiar with his sitter. His ability to convey the quiet authority of the monarch is without parallel in English royal portraiture – even Holbein's commanding study of Henry VIII and the highly wrought depictions of Elizabeth I lack this mixture of humanity and contrived distance. With extraordinary dexterity, Van Dyck has created the countenance of the king looking straight out, his deep-set eyes meeting those of the onlooker. Ingeniously the artist has enhanced the physical presence of his subject by slightly turning the body so that the armour, glinting in the sunlight, fills the lower half of the picture.

It is interesting to compare this portrait with a second image of Charles I, a marble bust by François Dieussart that stands in the adjacent corridor. It is another half-length of the king in his armour, yet there the similarities end. This is a more contemplative image and the sitter looks slightly troubled, avoiding the onlooker's gaze as if lost in thought. That said, the sculptor imbues the bust with life, contrasting the metallic severity of the armour with the almost wayward flamboyance of the king's hair and adding texture to the surface of the marble, creating curls here and folds there. This tousled naturalness reveals Dieussart's early training in Rome and his familiarity with the work of Bernini. The bust was part of a set of four commissioned by Lord Arundel, and one of its companions stands nearby, depicting the king's nephew Prince Charles Louis, Count Palatine of the Rhine. The other two, of the latter's brother, Prince Rupert, and of Lord Arundel himself, are now at the Ashmolean Museum in Oxford.

Collections rarely remain static, yet fortunately at Arundel works of art have tended to arrive rather than depart. Dieussart's busts were originally at Arundel House in the Strand and then Norfolk House in St James's Square before coming to the castle in the nineteenth century. Such movements can be traced in the extensive archives at Arundel, now fully investigated by the duke's indefatigable librarian, Dr John Martin Robinson. The eighteenth-century papers reveal that an enormous cultural debt is owed to Edward, 9th Duke (1686–1778), and his energetic wife Mary Blount, whose forthrightness occasioned her nickname 'My Lord Duchess'. They reassembled what remained of the early family collection, rebuilding both Norfolk House and Worksop Manor in Nottinghamshire and enhancing them with a series of brilliant purchases that today add to the glories

of Arundel Castle. The seat furniture now in the Drawing Room and Dining Room were made for Norfolk House in the 1750s by John Metcalfe, with covers from both the Soho Tapestry workshops and the duchess's own needlework. More spectacular still are the sideboards and pier tables, ordered for the London Dining Room, which demonstrate the sophistication of the duke and duchess's taste. Unique in English furniture of that time, they are made not of carved and gilded wood but of ormolu, a reflection of the origins of their designer, the Turinese architect Gian Battista Borra. The tables have black Derbyshire marble tops that contrast with the richly gilded metalwork beneath. The ormolu has been brilliantly worked so that the form and decoration seem to dissolve into one another; a hoof becomes the foot; a trellis entwined with vine leaves and grapes is the apron; and the whole composition is literally held together by crisply modelled goats' heads (all suitably Bacchic symbols for the ducal Dining Room). Vines even clamber up the walls to decorate the gilded frames that surround the matching pier glasses made by a fellow Turinese craftsman, J. A. Cuenot. Given their splendour, it is not surprising that after attending a celebratory party at Norfolk House, Horace Walpole noted: 'All the earth was there. You would have thought there had been a comet, everyone was gazing into the air and treading on one another's toes. In short you never saw such a scene of magnificence and taste'. Today the tables and glasses have been cleverly fitted into the Drawing Room at the castle, where their sheer audacity still stops you in your tracks, even in this unanticipated Gothic setting.

Above: *An architectural capriccio with an ecclesiastical building, part Pantheon and part St Mark's in Venice, by Canaletto.*

Opposite: *The exterior of Arundel Castle, circa 1770 by James Canter.*

In the adjacent Small Sitting Room are further examples of the Duke and Duchess's taste, this time three sparkling Canalettos. The artist had come to England in the mid 1740s in search of new patronage and over the following decade he would paint a series of ravishing scenes of London from the Thames, a reflection of his earlier work in Venice, and of country houses, a reflection of a particularly English passion. For the Norfolks, he was called on to paint something more unusual – a set of architectural capriccios. Familiar buildings, antique and Renaissance, are reconfigured to provide a dazzling backdrop for scenes of contemporary Italian life. In one, a group of figures are seen resting outside a church, part Roman Pantheon and part Doge's Chapel in Venice. In another, a troop of players set up their stage under an open loggia with Sansovino's Library and Cestius' tomb beyond. The lively imagination of these compositions is matched by the brio of the paintwork – Canaletto's brush seems never to settle too long as he deploys his palette of blues, pinks, yellows and bright greens. This is an artist at the height of his powers, responding to inspired patronage.

The duke and duchess looked elsewhere for strict topographical work. In 1777 they commissioned William Hodges to paint James Paine's vision for Worksop Manor, which was then being rebuilt to a grandiose Palladian design. Paine, their architect, had conceived a huge quadrangular palace to replace the Elizabethan house that had been destroyed by fire. If it had been finished (for it never was), it would have been the largest house built in England since Blenheim Palace. Comparing Hodges' picture of Worksop Manor, their principal country house, to a painting of Arundel shows how neglected the castle was at that time. James Canter's picture of the castle shows no architectural masterpiece, rather a hotch-potch of buildings, the ancient walls tamed by a medley of sash windows and a skyline of irregular pitched roofs. Since the sixteenth century the castle had become an estate backwater, where only occasional remedial work had been done. This was all set to change.

Building work at Worksop ceased after the 9th Duke's death in 1777 (the estate being later sold to the Duke of Newcastle in 1838), and his successors the 10th and 11th Dukes, distant cousins, turned their attention to Arundel. In 1787 Charles, 11th Duke of Norfolk, largely acting as his own architect, initiated a series of building projects that would still be incomplete upon his death in 1815. His unscholarly and wayward approach was not universally judged a success. Rather cruelly the professional architect J. C. Loudon wrote later: 'Arundel Castle . . . was for many years the scene of the late Duke of Norfolk's trials at building; by which as his own architect, he sought to instruct himself in the Gothic style. After being occupied in this way for upwards of forty years, and spending several hundred thousand pounds, he just arrived at last at the point where a man discovers his utter ignorance.' The scale of his work was prodigious and set the scene for the tide of rebuilding that followed. Not a stone remains of his building work but the series of paintings by William Daniel dating from the 1820s record his 'achievements'. The artist has clearly tried his best to disguise

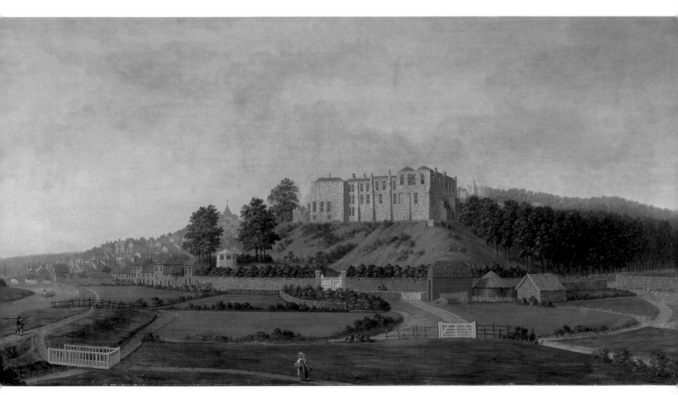

Above: *The Castle from Swanbourne Lake by William Daniell R.A., 1824.*

Opposite: *The Library designed by Henry Howard, 11th Duke of Norfolk with woodwork carved by Jonathan Ritson, father and son, in 1801.*

the gimcrack nature of the architecture, showing it in late-afternoon golden sunshine with screening trees and ivy climbing the walls. Even so the east and south fronts are revealed as monotonously regular, their features only slightly enlivened by 'cardboard' towers, and the internal courtyard was set about by buildings curiously piecemeal in approach. Internally though the 11th Duke's layout for Arundel largely survives, including his Library, created from the sixteenth-century Long Gallery in 1801, that today links the private apartments to the south wing.

Like many of the Duke's designs, the Library is a free interpretation of an historical precedent, in this case the perpendicular architecture found in St George's Chapel at Windsor. It was a bold decision to create a Regency Library based on a late-fifteenth-century ecclesiastical building, yet it works brilliantly. Two long 'naves' approach each other, replete with clustered columns and a ribbed vaulted ceiling. At the centre they intersect, at a crossing lit by a large Gothic window. The walls contain two tiers of Gothic bookcases, protected by brass grilles, the upper level being accessed by a gallery. The glinting brasswork is offset by the rich Honduras mahogany that encases the whole space and which is carved with delightful naturalistic ornament. It is one of the most attractive Regency libraries in the country, and it is no wonder it was spared from destruction during the century of rebuilding that followed. Indeed, it was improved by Morants, who provided a new carpet and curtains prior to Queen Victoria's visit in 1846. Whilst the originals wore out, their design survived in a watercolour by Catherine Lyons and this provided the basis for their recent restoration by the

present duchess. Morants also provided comfortable upholstered furniture which the duchess has returned to the Library, usefully identified by the maker's stamps on their undersides. Part of the ingenuity of the duke's Library is its capacity to store up to 10,000 books in a relatively small space. Many of the volumes formed part of the original eighteenth-century collections at Worksop Manor and Norfolk House, including a first edition of Mark Catesby's *Natural History of Carolina, Florida and the Bahama Islands* with its sumptuous colour plates depicting the exotic flora and fauna found there. These captured the imagination of many eighteenth-century collectors, including the Norfolks whose names are listed on the subscriber pages.

Walking from the Library to the State Rooms of the south wing, which the present duke and duchess are restoring, you enter again the realm of the 15th Duke and his architect Charles Alban Buckler. The Ante-Library is currently being repainted in a style more in keeping with the great heraldic fireplace and magnificent Gothic carved doorcase. The Drawing Room redecoration has already been completed. The walls have been washed in a greenish hue, a colour sympathetic to the oak ceiling and the hooded fireplace by Thomas Earp.

Above right: *George IV's coronation cup designed by Thomas Willement, made by Rundell & Brydges. It was presented to the 12th Duke of Norfolk who, as Earl Marshal, had arranged the monarch's sumptuous coronation.*

Opposite: *The redecorated Drawing Room showing the full-length 17th- and 18th-century portraits of members of the family.*

Strongly patterned fabrics have been used to enrich the architecture, often taking up colours from the painted heraldic shields that Buckler and his patron added liberally to these rooms. The aim has been to enhance the architecture and at the same time to restore the softening balance of earlier works of art. In the Drawing Room the new arrangement is so successful that you almost wonder how it can be achieved with such diverse pieces. Yet somehow the combination of portraits by Mytens, Van Dyck, Gainsborough and Reynolds, together with eighteenth-century furniture from England, France and Italy, works brilliantly against Buckler's interior, adapted from thirteenth-century architecture.

At the far end of the building is a space unchanged and unchanging, the Castle Chapel. It reaffirms the FitzAlan-Howards historic and continuing allegiance to the Catholic faith: a faith that has at times set them apart from the mainstream of British life and which has coloured their long history. It was built in the 1890s, towards the end of the 15th Duke's programme. Whilst his initial work had been carried out in the late 1870s, progress was halted when his duchess was diagnosed with a terminal disease. She died aged only 34 in 1887, and it seems thereafter that the duke turned back to his building work in search of solace. The foundation stone of the Chapel was laid in 1894, and it was completed four years later. It is both the summation of the duke's rebuilding of his ancestral castle and Buckler's masterpiece. He and his patron skilfully reinterpreted Henry III's lost Lady Chapel at Westminster Abbey (which was replaced by Henry VII's

Chapel) and through it evoked the enduring Catholicism of recusant England. The stained glass by Hardman's of Birmingham, inspired by the early English glass at Canterbury cathedral, recounts the life of the Virgin in deep and sonorous colours, whilst carved ceiling bosses in pale stone retell the same story along the ridgeline. Elsewhere slender columns of Purbeck marble and creamy Painswick stone soar up to capitals of naturalistic carving and spandrels containing bas reliefs of winged angels. There is an intensity of architectural and decorative expression here that reflects the 15th Duke's wish that his new building, the culmination of a century of work, should be of such quality in design and execution that it would last a thousand years. It is wearing well and, despite qualms as to its suitability as a house in the middle of the last century, it has shown itself both robust and adaptable. It fulfils those nineteenth-century dreams for a house commensurate with the family's history, and now incorpates the disparate works of art commissioned and collected by them over 400 years.

Berkeley Castle, Gloucestershire

The seat of the Berkeley Family

The great baronial families of England were largely destroyed by the Wars of the Roses. The civil war that broke out during the fifteenth century, as supporters of the rival houses of Lancaster and York pitted themselves against one another, saw the near extinction of the powerful feudal dynasties that had determined the fate of both England and a large part of France under Norman and Plantagenet kings. Names such as Mowbray, Mortimer and Bohun which resound through the history plays of Shakespeare disappeared, being replaced by the new families of the Tudor era: Cecil, Herbert and Russell. One of the few to have survived is Berkeley and, even more remarkably, John Berkeley and his family still live in the same castle that was given to his forebear Robert by Henry II in the mid 1100s.

Even before the twelfth century the strategic importance of the site was recognized, guarding on one side the mouth of the River Severn and, on the other, the main land route between Bristol to the south and Gloucester to the north. Before the Norman conquest this great manor was in the hands of Earl Godwin but with William I came a new feudal overlord, William FitzOsborn, his childhood friend. FitzOsborn, the Hereditary Steward of Normandy, was appointed to rule the western half of England in 1067. His principal task was to defend the land against a Welsh invasion establishing a line of castles from Hereford to Bristol to act as the bulwark of this defence. Today, with the softening of the landscape and the draining of the sea marshes, it is perhaps less easy to comprehend the castle's strategic position. Yet from the adjacent deer park you can readily see how it dominates the great sweep of the River Severn, with Lydney in the Forest of Dean on the far bank and beyond, to the south-west, Chepstow, Newport and Cardiff. The castle stands at the end of an outcrop of red rock, the ground falling away sharply on three sides, on a site originally further protected by boggy marshland. The only access was from the north, where the outcrop runs along a ridge on which the town of Berkeley would eventually be established. FitzOsborn took full advantage of his new home's geographical position. He raised a large earth mound on top of the outcrop to give increased visibility of the surrounding landscape and fortified this with a wooden stockade. An outer courtyard was built shortly afterwards and its form still sets the limit of the castle today, its palisaded walls following the edge of the outcrop, just to the point where it drops dramatically into the plain below.

Berkeley was well established by 1131 when Henry I was entertained here at Easter. But following the king's death four years later the internal struggles between his daughter Matilda and her cousin Stephen resulted in the FitzOsborns losing the castle. Matilda's son Henry of Anjou eventually became Henry II and he gave Berkeley to his supporter Robert Fitzharding, who became known as Robert, 1st Lord of Berkeley. The king also ordered the building of a new stone castle to replace FitzOsborn's wooden building. A new shell keep was raised, unusually enclosing the whole of the old mound, with walls sixty feet high that were strengthened by three semi-circular bastions. Although over the years its internal construction has changed, this keep is still largely intact. Standing beneath the castle today with young Charles Berkeley you can look up at those massive walls built of undressed local stone; a patchwork of pinks, purples, browns and creams – masonry that has survived since the twelfth century. The outer flanks, supported by buttresses, rise up, almost windowless to the crenelated battlements. High up in one of the semi-circular bastions is a surviving Norman window arch, which presumably lit one of the more important of the mid-twelfth-century rooms. Here, as elsewhere, are moments of architectural sophistication in an otherwise military building.

The contrast between military practicality and a desire for something more elaborate is best seen in the courtyard. A small doorway, approached by shallow steps, remains the only entrance to the castle from the ground floor. It is purposely restricted, the arched doorway leading to a steep flight of narrow stone steps – difficult to storm even if the building's outer defences had been breached. At their head is the internal doorway into the shell keep. Although worn over the years, its stonework reveals a master mason's hand. Its rounded arch is carved with a pattern of darts, with dogtooth decoration below, and to one side now stands a fat pilaster carved with a trellis pattern and topped by an intricate capital. This impressive piece of architecture reflects the work widespread in the royal palaces at that time, which is now known only through surviving Norman churches.

In the keep itself is another rare survival from this period: a small chapel lit by that sole surviving Norman window. Perched high in the tower, it is reached by a series of staircases that may account for its continued existence. Over the years it has been used for many purposes, but was restored in the twentieth century as the Chapel of St John and is still used today by the family. You enter obliquely and your eye is caught by the soaring ribs that hold up the barrel-vaulted ceiling. The plain stone walls to the sides are interrupted by a series of clustered columns that support the weight of the roof. At the far end there is a circular apse where the stone ribs descend on either side of a central window, creating a fan-shaped backdrop for the altar. Here hangs a great Romanesque painted wood crucifix, created in Italy around 1200, which was introduced here in the early 1930s.

Having been granted the castle, the Berkeley family grew in power and influence. Robert's grandson was amongst the barons who eventually forced King John to sign the Magna Carta, and his nephew Thomas, a prominent military leader, became Vice-Constable of England in 1297. Thomas's son Maurice (1281–1326) held a series of important royal appointments during the early years of Edward II's reign but his opposition to the king's favourite, Hugh Despencer, led to his imprisonment in Wallingford Castle in 1322 where he died four years later. Maurice's eldest son, Thomas, was also incarcerated, at Pevensey Castle, but following his father's death he was released. This was no simple act of mercy but a reflection that any loyalty to King Edward could be discounted. England was at the brink of civil war and Thomas Berkeley had a particular part to play in its resolution.

Opposite: The Norman doorway with carved arch and pilaster in the Castle Keep.

Above: *The Internal Courtyard, showing from the left the Kitchen Block, the entrance to the Great Hall, one of the Great Hall windows, the new entrance front with Gothic doorcase (inserted circa 1925) and, to the right, the late 14th-century domestic quarters, now containing the Drawing Room.*

Edward II's reign should have been a success. The young king inherited a stable kingdom from his father Edward I and his dynastic marriage to Isabella of France should have secured his French territories. However, his penchant for favouring young courtiers, first Piers Gaverston (who met his end on a gallows on Blacklow Hill in 1312) and then Hugh Despencer, was strongly resented by both the barons and Queen Isabella. By 1325 they were in open rebellion to depose the king, planning to supplant him with his eldest son Prince Edward. That autumn, the queen and her lover Roger Mortimer successfully forced Edward to flee to the west, where he was captured at Llantrisant in south Wales. The Despencers, father and son, were executed whilst the king was whisked away to imprisonment in Kenilworth Castle. Here in January 1326 he was forced to abdicate in favour of his young son Edward III.

The deposed monarch was inevitably the subject of intrigue and plotting. In order to minimize this risk, Mortimer decided he should be sent to a more remote spot. Mortimer, father of Thomas Berkeley's wife, may well have put pressure on his son-in-law (who had just been released from Pevensey) to take the royal prisoner to Berkeley. In April 1326 Edward arrived at the castle, never to leave. He was most likely kept in a small room above the stairs to the keep – certainly this is the room now traditionally associated with his end. Various plots to free him were hatched during the summer and this may have hardened the resolve of his captors, who decided that the former monarch had to die. They hoped that the terrible smell from rotting animal carcasses, thrown into a great charnel pit adjacent to his cell, would cause his death through asphyxiation. But Edward was still young and fit and did not succumb.

By September the barons decided more drastic acts were needed and Thomas Berkeley saw fit to quit the castle leaving Edward in the care of his gaolers. Their task was to dispatch their former king in a way that would leave no trace on his body and it is probable that he was suffocated on 21 September, although a rumour started to circulate shortly afterwards that his death had been infinitely more painful and gruesome, with claims that his internal organs had been burnt out with a red hot poker forced up his backside. If this was so, Thomas Gray's words are horridly appropriate: *'The shrieks of death thro' Berkeley's roof that ring / Shrieks of an agonizing King'*. On 22 October the embalmed remains of Edward II were taken with all ceremony to Gloucester to lie in state for a month before being interred in the cathedral. A great canopy tomb, one of the finest in Europe, was erected by the royal masons with an alabaster effigy of the monarch resting on a tomb chest made of Purbeck marble. His supposed prison cell at Berkeley also remains dedicated to the memory of this unfortunate monarch – a plain room now lined with rush matting and simply furnished.

Thomas, Lord Berkeley himself, has a splendid tomb in the nearby church of St Mary's, lying next to his second wife, Katherine Cliveden. He died in 1361, having been acquitted by Edward III of any involvement in his father's death.

He served his new king in France as Marshall of the English Army and fought at the battle of Crécy in 1346, and in death he is shown as a mighty warrior: his face ensconced in an open helmet, his body clad in armour and his great sheathed sword hanging from an elaborate belt. He and his wife gaze eternally at the roof of the church in prayer. Thomas was responsible for rebuilding this church and also transformed his castle, building a fine sequence of new rooms in the latest Gothic style. The barrel-vaulted ceilings, rounded arches and thick columns of his predecessors were replaced by lofty roofs and pointed arches. His new buildings included the Great Hall, a range of kitchens and the new Chapel of St Mary. Berkeley is one of very few domestic buildings in England where you can contrast early Norman domestic architecture and the light ebullience of the new Gothic.

The cell traditionally thought to be where Edward II was murdered.

In the Great Hall, the comparison could not be clearer. On the outer wall are three deep Norman embrasures with beautifully modelled rounded arches, preserved from an earlier hall, and opposite are pairs of lofty Gothic windows, headed by trefoil arched tops. These are surmounted by four great segmental arches which also appear on the doorcases: these 'Berkeley' arches are of such a distinct form that they have given their name to the shape itself. The best of these Gothic arches is seen around the massive door that leads up to Thomas's new chapel; a half-octagon that tick-tocks around, lightened by an internal running pattern reminiscent of clover leaves. The Great Hall is unusually large and its massive timber roof was cleverly constructed with a saddle-like top resting on arched braces, rather than rising to an apex as was the norm. Beneath, the room extends from a screen up to the dais where the family and guests would take their meals. A great fire would originally have smouldered away in the centre, its smoke drifting up to one of the two flues in the roof. So much of this building has remained intact that you can quite understand the sentiments of the current owner, John Berkeley, when he says, standing in the hall of his ancestors, that you acutely feel the past and the slow passage of time.

Opposite: The Great Hall built by Thomas the Magnificent, showing the Berkeley Arch above the doorway and window.

Whilst John is a direct descendant of Thomas, Lord Berkeley, his line stems from a younger son whose descendants moved to Spetchley in Worcestershire in the late sixteenth century. They inherited the castle in the 1940s when the last Earl of Berkeley died. John's father was such a distant cousin that the connection lay back in the fifteenth century, with Thomas Berkeley of Dursley (born c.1440). The Spetchley Berkeleys knew their cousins as the Castle Berkeleys — a term John still uses, particularly when referring to the main point of difference between the two. The Castle Berkeleys converted to Protestantism whereas their Spetchley cousins remained true to the Catholic faith of their ancestors. The chapel that Thomas built in the late fourteenth century was a sign of that faith acknowledged in 1364 when Pope Urban V granted 'a forty day indulgence to all those who worship or make benefactions to the Chapels of the Blessed Virgin Mary and St John in Berkeley Castle'. It has since become the Morning Room but much of its original decoration survives. It is easy to imagine how the altarpiece would have looked at the far end. It would have been approached by two aisles, the narrow outer one carved out of the solid Norman wall and pierced by two apertures headed by more Berkeley arches. Above the altar, the roof timbers sprang from carved bosses halfway up the walls, forming elongated trefoil shapes as they stretched out to support the roof beams themselves. What is really remarkable is that the original paintwork on the ceiling beams is still visible, retaining its lively vibrant colours and reminding us how much Gothic decoration was painted. They are also painted with texts derived from the Book of Revelation, not though in Latin (as would have been usual) but in Norman French. This was devised by John Trevisa, who became chaplain at Berkeley to Thomas's grandson, another Thomas, who inherited in 1368. Trevisa, like his contemporary William Wyclif, believed that it was important for the church to adopt the lay language of its congregation and translated the Bible into Norman French. He was expelled from Oxford University for this act in 1379, and found refuge at Berkeley soon after. Appropriately, the Morning Room also houses one of the illuminated manuscripts belonging to the family, a great antiphon from which monks would have sung plain chant. The notated staves and words, broken into syllables, were illuminated to a large scale so that a group of singers

Above: *The east end of the Morning Room, formerly the Chapel of St Mary, showing the painted Gothic wooden ceiling.*

Opposite: *The Medieval Kitchen with its series of large ranges and high timber roof.*

gathered round a single lectern could read them with ease. The Gothic delight in painted decoration is echoed here; the pages inked in a variety of colours, with the initials often illuminated with large scenes taken from the New Testament.

Thomas, like his grandfather, was a soldier, serving in the wars in France, Spain, Brittany and Scotland. He was also immensely wealthy, having inherited through his wife, Margaret, the great de Lisle estates in 1382. Four years later he entertained Richard II at Berkeley, when the Great Hall and adjacent kitchens added by his grandfather must have proved invaluable. Incredibly, these kitchens have also survived. Their scale is truly impressive, particularly the scullery with its soaring stone beams where originally an open conduit would have carried the rubbish outside the castle's walls. The adjacent kitchen occupies the whole of a hexagonal tower, rising over three floors to a criss-cross patterned timbered roof. There are three huge open grates where the food would have been cooked on spits. Those cooks must have been grateful for the sheer height of the room, which allowed the heat to rise up, and for the very tall chimney stacks which let the smoke disperse with no danger of it being blown back down.

Living in a building with its medieval rooms intact presents some problems. Castles of that time did not contain drawing rooms, dining rooms, bedrooms or bathrooms. Over the years at Berkeley such rooms have been created, yet it is nevertheless true that John's sons, Charles and Henry, had when young either to cross the courtyard, run up the keep's steps and through the Norman portal, or go to the top of the south range, cross the old drawbridge and then drop down a spiral staircase to get to their beds! Likewise John's wife, Gina, works in a kitchen in an undercroft. Fortunately it has a handy door into the courtyard so each morning she can slip outside with her huge Newfoundland, Kittywake.

Few alterations took place in the fifteenth and sixteenth centuries as a result of family wrangling over the inheritance. These disagreements culminated when William, Lord Berkeley (1426–1492), Great Marshall of England, left the castle to King Henry VII and his male heirs in return for being made a marquess. This decision prevented his brother Maurice and his descendants from owning Berkeley until the death of Edward VI (the last of Henry VII's male heirs) in 1553 when the castle reverted to the family. The sixteenth-century Berkeleys secured their fortune through a series of great dynastic marriages: Henry, Lord Berkeley (1534–1615), marrying Lady Catherine Howard, daughter of Lord Surrey, and their son Thomas marrying Elizabeth Carey, daughter and sole heir of Lord Hunsdon (Elizabeth I's cousin). The fine portrait of her father, by the court painter Marcus Gheeraerts, now hangs in the Great Hall. He stands resplendent in fashionable black doublet and hose, his cloak stitched with gold thread and his cap studded with jewels. It was through Elizabeth Carey, Lady Berkeley, that the family gained a second great house. In 1618, some time after her husband's death, she bought Cranford in Middlesex from the heirs of Sir Roger Aston. This large house near London continued to be used by the family, in tandem with the castle, until the mid twentieth century. Now demolished, its site is largely taken by Heathrow airport, but you can still see the brick stable buildings as you drive out of London along the M4 towards Windsor.

George, Lord Berkeley, son of Thomas and Elizabeth, held Berkeley during the English Civil War. The strategic military importance that had first attracted FitzOsborn meant the castle could not be overlooked by either side. It was initially taken by the Parliamentarians but then fell to the king's army. In 1645 the

Parliamentary forces returned, quickly taking the town and the church, but the castle held out for three more days. Then, with no hope of any Royalist relief, it was surrendered. The siege appears to have been extremely good natured and the opposing forces left the building largely undamaged: just a slice of the old keep wall was demolished. This may have been a result of George's own gentle disposition. The epitaph on his tomb declares he had a 'singular bounty and affability towards his inferiors and [a] readiness (had it been within his power) to have obliged all mankind'.

His son, another George (1627–1698), was among the six peers who invited Charles II to return, visiting the exiled monarch in The Hague in 1660. This was a rare political act in a life largely devoted to restoring his family's financial position. His immediate predecessors had spent without thought and the family steward, John Smith, told him in 1645 that the estates would soon be worth less than 'your great-great-grandfather's yearly expended in livery cotes [sic] and badges'. One of his first steps was to court a rich lady, and one with good commercial connections. He could not have chosen better. The following summer he married Elizabeth, daughter and heir of John Massingberd, who was treasurer of the East India Company. George's subsequent involvement in trade with the burgeoning new colonies was to last his lifetime. He followed his own private interests as well, serving on various boards including that of Trade and Plantations, the Royal African Company and the Levant Company, of which he was the governor from 1673 to 1696. His diligence paid off and by 1677 the financial position of his estates had been secured. His personal wealth then was reckoned at £26,000; with £8,000 alone in East India stock. At the same time, his standing at court remained high, and in 1679 Charles II raised him to the earldom of Berkeley and viscountcy of Dursley.

Opposite: The Picture Gallery showing the portrait of Admiral Lord Berkeley and in the foreground on the table the dockyard model of a ship of the line.

His son Charles, later 2nd Earl of Berkeley (1649–1710), followed his father's mercantile lead, also serving on the committees of the Levant and East India companies. He is probably responsible for acquiring some of the more exotic works of art in the castle. These include rare ebony chairs, made in India towards the end of the seventeenth century, and the striking (although anonymous) *Panorama of Constantinople*. Here is a scene which bustles with activity as foreign merchants trade with the Ottoman Turks, their ships moored in the Golden Horn. These merchants dealt in luxury goods, satisfying the taste in Europe for things as novel then as coffee, tea, silks and oriental porcelain. The fine pair of contemporary paintings attributed to Jacob Knyff hanging in the Picture Gallery show exactly the sort of vessels used by these merchants when trading across continents.

In the same room hang paintings of the next Earl of Berkeley, James (c.1680–1723), and his cousins Charles and John (both Lords Berkeley of Stratton). They are all depicted as naval officers with their vessels in the distance, for just as the family was deeply involved in the expansion of trade, it was also closely bound

up with the development of the English navy. James, 3rd Earl of Berkeley, first saw action under Admiral Rooke, commanding *The Boyne* off Malaga in 1704. He subsequently rose to become Vice-Admiral of England and Master of Trinity House. In a great painting by William van de Velde I (also in the Gallery), you get a sense of the ships they commanded, first when confronting the Dutch and then the French fleets in the late seventeenth century. Here the great flagship of Charles, Lord Berkeley of Stratton, *The Tyger*, is shown in the centre, with his flag as Admiral of the Red fluttering at its stern. High up on the central mast the Royal Standard is also flown, indicating that Charles II is on board. Bobbing around on the choppy sea are numerous smaller vessels, some firing salutes to celebrate their monarch and his refurbishment of the English fleet. On the long table in the centre of the same room is a spectacular dockyard model of a ship of the line. Executed in fruitwood and ivory, it must have been made around 1720 and was probably ordered by James, who by then had been appointed First Lord of the Admiralty. This boat is stripped down to the essentials, proudly display-ing the latest in naval technology and design. The model is exquisitely executed

with equal attention to detail and decoration – the sides with a painted frieze of sea horses and stylized beasts whilst the stern displays the royal monogram GR (for Georgius Rex). The portholes on its sides can be lifted to reveal rows of cannon.

The Berkeley family's involvement in the navy was to continue throughout the eighteenth century. One of the greatest portraits in the collection, a master-piece by Thomas Gainsborough, celebrates the achievements of the 4th Earl's grandson, Sir George Cranford Berkeley (1753–1818). He is shown as a young officer in the mid 1780s, standing with his naval sword aloft, his courage and audacity brilliantly captured by the artist. Behind the sitter, Gainsborough (who never went to sea) has employed his brushes to great effect, cleverly evoking the strength and frenzy of the oceans with Berkeley's small vessel tossed among mighty waves. Sir George had served under both his cousin Admiral Keppel and John Jervis, later Lord St Vincent. Around the time this portrait was painted, he married his distant cousin, Lady Emma Charlotte Lennox from Goodwood.

The collection abounds in fine full-length portraits of the family painted during the eighteenth century, including those by Gavin Hamilton of Augustus, 4th Earl, and his wife, Elizabeth Drax. She was noted for her dexterity with a needle, and the splendid covers to the suite of gilt-seat furniture in the Long Drawing

Room show just how skilled she was. The portrait of their son Frederick by Pompeo Batoni hangs in the same room. This shows the young man in Rome wearing a splendid scarlet jacket, cream waistcoat and breeches pointing out the classical ruins. It bounces with energy and captures his 'hell for leather' attitude which would eventually lead to the Berkeley succession being upset once again. He inherited whilst still young, being just ten when his father died, and after his Grand Tour returned to join the army and indulge his passion for the chase.

Left: *Admiral Sir George Cranfield Berkeley (1754–1818) by Thomas Gainsborough R.A.*

Hunting seems always to have been part of life at Berkeley. Records show that even in 1326 (when Edward II was there as a prisoner) Thomas, Lord Berkeley, was breeding hounds. Over 200 years later his descendant, Henry Berkeley (1534–1618), was much criticized for spending 'near three parts of the year . . . in hunting the hare, fox and deere [sic]'. The great walled deer park to the south west of the castle belongs to his time: the nearby stables (built in the Gothick style) from 200 years later, built by the 5th Earl (1745–1810). Both the hunters and hounds were well housed in a series of buildings including loose boxes, stores for hay and straw, and exercise yards. Here, in that practical eighteenth-century way, rainwater was collected from the roofs, running through large lead

pipes to feed stone troughs, providing a source of fresh drinking water for the animals. The stable woodwork is still painted mustard and green, the colours as worn by the Berkeley huntsmen and taken from the household livery — outdoor (mustard) and indoor (green). The Berkeley Vale remains home to the Berkeley Hunt, and the huntsmen still wear this distinctive attire. The hunt is today led by John Berkeley's younger son, Henry, who modestly claims to be less well turned out than his kinsman Randal, 8th and last Earl of Berkeley, who liked to wear a bunch of violets in his lapel — such a good contrasting colour to the mustard yellow! Not surprisingly there are a number of portraits of the hunt servants around the castle but the most beautiful of these sporting painting has to be that by George Stubbs, ARA, which was surely commissioned by the 5th Earl. A chestnut and a dapple-grey hunter stand beneath a great tree whilst a groom approaches with a feeding tray. It is early morning and these finely bred animals, every muscle and bone beautifully expressed, stand against a cool pink-grey sky.

This is one of Stubbs' mature masterpieces, revealing his ability not only to depict horses accurately but also to portray their individual temperaments.

Frederick clearly had a passionate nature. Unlike his forebears, who often married for dynastic or financial reasons, he followed his heart. He fell passionately in love with young Mary Cole, the daughter of a butcher at nearby Wotton-under-Edge. The portrait of her by John Hoppner, painted in the 1790s, shows a delicate, pretty girl, observant and intelligent. She became first Frederick's mistress and then his wife. She lived principally at Berkeley until her husband's death in 1810, where she involved herself with the estate and became extremely popular among the local people. She became the patroness of a local doctor, Edward Jenner, allowing him to use a thatched building in the Chantry Garden as his laboratory.

It was here that he developed the serum for inoculations against smallpox. She and Lord Berkeley had a bevy of children; some born in wedlock and others not. Lord Berkeley, in a rather cavalier mood, tried to legitimize all his offspring by doctoring the local marriage records but after his death the House of Lords would have none of it. Their eldest four sons were deemed illegitimate and so the earldom passed to the fifth, the first born after their marriage in 1796. However, the Berkeleys had agreed that rather than bar the eldest son, William, from his inheritance, the title should effectively go into abeyance.

During the nineteenth century the castle was first owned by William (who was created Earl Fitzhardinge) and after him by further descendants of the 5th Earl, but in 1916 the whole of this line failed. The heir to the estate was a 50-year-old widower, Randal Berkeley, great-grandson of Gainsborough's naval hero Sir George Cranfield Berkeley. Although he too had served as a naval officer in his

Opposite: *A bay and a dappled grey hunter with groom in the Berkeley livery by George Stubbs A.R.A.*

Left: *Mary Cole, Countess of Berkeley, by John Hoppner.*

early years, his principal interest was science and he lived, surrounded by laboratories, just outside Oxford. However, on becoming Earl, he turned his attention fully to his inheritance and with energy, flair and money raised through the sale of the family's London estates, in his own words set to work 'to transform the castle into the most beautiful in England'.

For the next decade the courtyards rang with the sounds of building work. His American second wife, Mary Lowell, whom he married in 1924, recalled that he had an absolute mania for building: 'If you went away for a few days, you'd come back to find the side of your room taken off and all the furniture moved out'. His aim was to reveal the ancient beauty of the building. He replaced lost elements, such as the screen in the Great Hall with a fifteenth-century screen from Cefn Mably in Wales. He also removed the jarring additions made over the previous two centuries, including the panelling from the Long Drawing Room walls. His other object was to bring the castle up to date, tactfully introducing modern conveniences. The principal guest bedroom has hardly changed since he and his decorators, Keeble & Co., had transformed it to create a perfect castle bedroom. The walls, painted a stone colour, are hung with tapestries and rich Spanish leather work, a suitable backdrop for the great late-sixteenth-century tester bed. This he had had carefully restored; the ancient layers of dead polish were removed and sixteenth-century style crewelwork hangings and a comfortable mattress were added. A Mortlake tapestry was turned into a screen whilst an Italian walnut table became a writing surface with an adjustable wrought-iron light hanging above.

The introduction of electricity was ingenious. All manner of objects were transformed into lamps and when Lord Berkeley could not find a period object to adapt (as in this room), Keeble's would create something suitable. Such historical exactitude is less visible in the bathrooms he added, some being carved out of the thickness of the walls. In one case an entire bathroom, which Lord and Lady Berkeley had admired at the Waldorf Astoria Hotel in New York, was purchased, shipped across the Atlantic and installed on an upper floor. This is a feast of yellow and black marble, topped by a classical bronze frieze.

To the exterior of the castle, Lord Berkeley replaced some sixty windows with more suitable Gothic alternatives, and he even introduced the octagonal porch in the centre of the courtyard. (His agents found this in France and had it shipped over.) The original coat of arms was re-carved and now the two wild men hold aloft the Berkeley arms. Here as elsewhere his work now sits comfortably alongside the original medieval building. Lord Berkeley's aspirations have been achieved. Berkeley Castle is indeed one of the most beautiful medieval buildings in England. Even more, it remains home to the family who will celebrate the 900th anniversary of the royal gift in just a few decades' time.

Burghley House, Lincolnshire

The seat of the Marquesses of Exeter

In the late seventies I was travelling with a colleague who suggested we might stay the night with Simon and Lady Victoria Leatham at their house near Alconbury. We arrived after dark but I can recall the hilltop house, lights blazing, an opening door, a rush of enthusiastic dogs and beaming Leatham smiles. After dinner, talk turned to work and Victoria said that she longed for something to do, ideally in the art world. Her children were growing up, Simon was working in London and she did not just want to look after the house. Within months she had joined Sotheby's, learning about works of art on the trot. She took to it naturally, enjoying the camaraderie of fellow enthusiasts and the excitement of finding the unexpected. Her passion for art should have come as no surprise for, as the youngest daughter of the Marquess of Exeter, she had grown up at Burghley, the family's ancestral home. The house was almost walled with paintings bought in the seventeenth and eighteenth centuries and her early visual companions had been masterpieces by Italians such as Guercino and Gentileschi, as well as the great series of frescoes by Antonio Verrio.

Life was about to turn full circle. Having in part escaped the daily routine of looking after the house at Alconbury, Victoria found herself looking after a much bigger house, Burghley itself.

When her father died in 1981 a preservation trust was established to ensure the future of the house and its collection. One of the trust's stipulations was that a member of the family should live there, and Simon and Victoria were chosen. It is one thing to grow up in a house – you at least know its geography – but it is quite another to have the responsibility of looking after it. Walking through the rooms today it is difficult to imagine what confronted the family: a plethora of buckets catching rainwater from leaking ceilings; the threads that trailed from old faded fabrics; cupboards stuffed full of objects that had not seen the light of day for years, perhaps even centuries. At times it must have seemed daunting, but the excitement of each new discovery and putting that object back into its rightful context drove them on. I remember the buzz as ancient tapestries, stored in the old night nurseries, were pulled out and unfurled on the antechapel floor to reveal an explosion of colour: and old wooden chests opened to reveal not the expected domestic china, but eighteenth-century scientific instruments. Elsewhere early Japanese ceramics emerged which were later matched with those recorded in an inventory drawn up for the 5th Earl in 1688.

Like a great jigsaw puzzle, every piece had a place and it was just a matter of fitting it all together. You can now trace Burghley's history through its architecture and works of art, from its inception in the mid sixteenth century to the last significant alterations that took place in the nineteenth century. Its creator, William Cecil, 1st Lord Burghley (1521–1598), would be delighted. He set out to create a building that would survive forever; and one synonymous with his family name and after 500 years all is going well.

As the name Cecil implies, the family originated in Wales. David Cecil joined Henry Tudor's army and became one of the new king's bodyguards after the battle of Bosworth. Through a relative he came to live in Stamford and represented the town in Parliament. He secured a position as Page to the Chamber to Henry VIII for his son Richard, who advanced the family's position at court, and in Lincolnshire through his marriage to Jane Heckington, whose dowry included the lordship of Burghley. Their son, William Cecil, was born in 1521 and after studying at Stamford and Grantham entered St John's College Cambridge in 1535. Here he mastered Latin, Greek, French, Italian and Spanish as well as studying logic, so developing an ability to reach balanced judgements. This was to become his hallmark; his numerous surviving memoranda demonstrate how he would pose a question and then list out the pros and cons before arriving at the optimal solution. Such a rational approach was later to stand him in good stead as a minister of state, and as a builder.

After Cambridge and studying law at Gray's Inn, Cecil entered Protector Somerset's service in 1547. After Somerset's fall he was briefly imprisoned in the Tower of London. On his release, he kept a low profile until emerging at the end of Queen Mary's reign as the trusted servant of the young Princess Elizabeth. On 17 November 1558, the first day of Elizabeth I's reign, she appointed the 37-year-old Cecil her Secretary of State. He was to serve her until his death forty years later, becoming Lord High Treasurer in 1572. The previous year he had been created Lord Burghley, joining that very small and select group of hereditary peers, and was subsequently created a Knight of the Garter. His activities as a builder can be seen as a celebration of his preferment as well as the incarnation in stone of his dynastic aspiration for his two sons. His ambitions were to be realized in the survival of the eldest son's line at Burghley, first as Earls and then Marquesses of Exeter, and of his second son's at Hatfield, as Earls and later Marquesses of Salisbury.

Burghley is one of the largest Elizabethan mansions ever built. Originally with two wings projecting to the north (one of these was taken down in the eighteenth century), the rest survives. Building work commenced in the 1550s and the west front (the original entrance front) remains largely as Lord Burghley would have known it. In the centre it is a tall tower rising over four floors and topped with polygonal turrets, matched by further turrets at either end of the façade. There is a pleasing symmetry to the design as well as an exuberant strength and grandeur. Just think how it must have seemed to a traveller passing by on the old Great North Road in the sixteenth century.

You enter the building through a large arch in the centre, flanked by sturdy bare walls with two classical niches set in the spandrels, and proceed directly into his Entrance Hall. Here the floor is strongly patterned in black and white marble and the walls, like those outside, are of plain cut stone. The stone ceiling has a wonderful rich Gothic vault of intersecting arches, with Burghley's newly created arms in the centre. This work is in contrast to the classical decoration above the entrance arches with their patterns of squares and circles. Beyond, through a second smaller hall that originally led on either side to open arcades, is the inner courtyard. Lord Burghley's decision to use the same stone here as outside cleverly disguises the transition from the reality of the outside world into the fantasy of his internal courtyard.

Lord Burghley's portrait hangs in the Entrance Hall as if still overseeing his building. It shows him as an old man, beady-eyed, modest in stance, proud in his Garter robes and holding his staff as Lord Treasurer in his right hand. He was Queen Elizabeth's astute chief minister who guided her through the thorny problems of her reign, including those surrounding Mary, Queen of Scots and the Spanish Armada. At the time this portrait was painted, he and his son Robert had in effect become her government, as other leading courtiers had died: the Earl of Leicester in 1588, Sir Francis Walsingham in 1590 and Sir Christopher Hatton in 1591. Lady Victoria points out that Lord Burghley's cardinal virtue was his total honesty – indeed, the queen charged him that he should never lie to her. Even if they disagreed on which policy to adopt, monarch and servant were equally aware of how matters stood. It was a rare long-lasting trust that stood both Elizabeth and Lord Burghley in good stead.

The Inner Courtyard was the pinnacle of Lord Burghley's architectural achievements and it has survived intact. The symmetry of the west façade is maintained but here enlivened by all manner of devices. The ground floor, with its arcades,

supports four grand central arches on the first floor, showing a debt to the classical language employed on Protector Somerset's house in London in the mid sixteenth century. However, here the walls are so engulfed by all manner of decorative motifs that it becomes a triumphant Elizabethan hybrid. The space rises to a climax at the far end. Here stands a second entrance, flanked by niches and set between columns. On the two floors above, these architectural devices are repeated, with the upper storey centred on a large casement window. Above this is set a clock, dated 1573, wrapped round by Lord Burghley's Garter and seemingly held in place by huge rampant lions, his armorial supporters. Finally, the whole is surmounted by a weighty pyramid topped with a ball.

Overawed by this spectacle, the visitor would pass through the second entrance and up a flight of steps to reach Lord Burghley's most extravagant room, the

Great Hall. It has changed little since it was built in the 1570s, save for the rather florid bookcases that were introduced in the nineteenth century to accommodate the library overflow. As with the decoration elsewhere, the Hall is a delicious mixture of late Gothic and early classical styles. The great double hammer-beam roof, built of local timber, runs to a majestic height. Its shape and construction follow traditional late medieval lines, albeit on a huge scale, whilst its decoration incorporates stone corbels, lions' heads, profile portraits and a medley of classical ornament. These would have made it startlingly original to an Elizabethan onlooker, exactly as Lord Burghley intended. He was both a traditionalist and a forward thinker, his logical training allowing him to hold both in balance. There is a respect, even an evocation, of the past coupled with an excitement of the new architectural forms that he encountered in his Italian and French architectural tomes.

There is a family story that Elizabeth I intended to visit Lord Burghley's new house. If this is true, it might not only have been the anticipated expenses of a royal visit that led him to seek to deflect her, but also royal criticism of his architectural flamboyance. It is said that whilst she was making her progress northwards, Lord Burghley devised a way to deter her from visiting. He waited until the last minute before

sending a messenger scurrying south with the news that he feared his daughter had contracted smallpox. It worked a treat, and the queen and her expensive retinue deflected elsewhere.

On one side of his Great Hall is the swagger stone fireplace. Its outline reflects the courtyard's pyramid tower though the upper part is curved rather than triangular and rises to a bold pediment. In the centre Lord Burghley's arms are proudly displayed, crisply carved and so well executed that the tails of the lion supporters stand proud as if just swished into place. Beneath is a richly carved mantle with an interlaced ribbon pattern held steady by succulent carved leaves. The whole is amusingly secured by the swelling ribbed jambs topped with small rosettes teetering on small paws.

Burghley's architecture seldom lacks panache and this is true even of the stone staircase that rises from the ground floor out onto the roof. Called the Roman Staircase, it incorporates the classical decoration seen in the entrance arches and expanded here to cover the barrel-vaults of each flight. It is the proportion of this beautifully orchestrated *tour de force* that captivates. Everything – the ornament, the scale of the treads, and the incised handrail – is subservient to it. Your measured progress up to the roof gives such pleasure, only to be followed by a shock. Having become accustomed to the decorum of the stairs, the roofscape looks as if someone has run amok with building blocks. In fact, everything is brilliantly thought through yet the vastness of the space and the sheer number of ornamental incidents do suggest an architectural riot from certain angles.

For the Elizabethans, the pleasure of a house did not end with the rooms but continued on to the roof. Here you could take exercise, meet people privately and even take meals whilst enjoying the views. It could also provide an area for architectural fireworks like those achieved at Burghley. It is a fantasy where

Opposite: *The Great Hall with Lord Burghley's Great Fireplace containing his coat of arms.*

Above: *A view of the roof showing the riot of architectural details.*

triple Tuscan columns form chimneys that are linked at the top for stability and then crowned by small armorial castles. Elsewhere gilded pennants fly from the tops of cupolas, obelisks stand on open arches, some flanked by stone balls with twisted metal spikes, and richly carved shells standing on brackets surmount non-existent windows. The void of the courtyard below makes the whole seem more fantastical, with the sense that you could easily leave this architectural paradise by falling over a parapet. Today an accident is more likely since the roof pitch has been steepened since the sixteenth century. The tower reaches its full height above the Entrance Hall, providing a single room for observation and perhaps banquets. Reached by either the long spiral staircase from the ground floor or small doors from the roof, it now has the pleasant mustiness of a lumber room. Lord Burghley's thoughtfulness to his guests extends, even here, to the inclusion in the far corner of a tiny privy.

Lord Burghley's enterprise and cultural enthusiasm would not re-emerge until the end of the seventeenth century with his great-great-great grandson, John

Opposite and left: John Cecil, 5th Earl of Exeter (1648–1700) and Lady Anne Cavendish, Countess of Exeter both by Sir Godfrey Kneller, Bt.

Lord John Cecil, later 6th Earl of Exeter (1674–1721) by Willem Wissing.

Cecil, 5th Earl of Exeter (1648–1700). He was the son of the 4th Earl and his wife, Lady Frances Manners, through whom he was related to the Earls of Rutland and the Lords Montagu. His own marriage in 1670 to Lady Anne Cavendish made him brother-in-law to the 1st Duke of Devonshire. He was thus intimately connected with the leading patrons of the arts of late-seventeenth-century England. The roll call of the houses they rebuilt and lavishly furnished conjures up the baroque movement – Belvoir Castle in Leicestershire, Montagu House in Bloomsbury, Boughton in Northamptonshire and perhaps, above all, Chatsworth in Derbyshire. It is not surprising that the 5th Earl and his Countess decided that Burghley was looking distinctly old-fashioned and in need of attention. Even so, their internal remodelling is startling in both its scale and grandeur.

The new earl inherited in 1678 and shortly after took advantage of the damage caused by Parliamentarian troops in the Civil War to remodel the south front. Approaching it today his intervention remains clear. He filled in Lord Burghley's ground floor arcade and inserted a huge baroque doorcase in the centre. This is surmounted by a large robust cartouche containing his arms, quartered with those of his Cavendish wife, to emphasize that this was his house and his work. The door leads into his Marble Hall with its prodigious plaster ceiling, panelled walls and marble floor. Hanging in the far corner is Kneller's sensitive portrait of this young man, wearing a fashionably full wig, tight-fitting coat and cloak. A portrait of his young wife, Lady Anne, also by Kneller, hangs to his left.

The room, which originally contained his marble sculptures (hence its name), is now lined with family portraits. The most flamboyant is that of the earl's eldest son, another John, who would become 6th Earl of Exeter in 1700. He was born in Kensington in 1674, and this fine portrait was painted about a decade later by the Dutchman Willem Wissing, a favourite artist of his father. He is shown as a young sportsman, fowling piece in hand and dog at his side. Wissing's colours have a slight but pleasing astringency. To emphasize the portrait's importance it is surrounded by an exuberant carved oak frame in the manner of Grindling Gibbons, who is also recorded as working for the 5th Earl. Here the wood is delicately carved to create putti, flowers, fruit and hanging game, with bees buzzing around shells and even a long rope of intertwined pearls – the baroque style at its most flamboyant and engaging.

On either side of the Marble Hall lay the earl and countess's apartments. Although now somewhat remodelled, the family's private Red Drawing Room still retains its original gilded plaster ceiling with the central flat area treated to ever more elaborate borders as it expands out to the walls. In the corners are huge pendant wreaths of flowers skirted by swirls of foliage. The room is now thickly hung with pictures including Carlo Maratta's *Christ and the Woman from Samaria* and Carlo Dolci's deliciously rich *Adoration of the Magi*, which were probably both acquired by the 5th Earl in Italy in 1681. The large *Venus and Adonis* by Baciccio is likely to have been a slightly later purchase as it does not appear on their 1688 inventory.

That inventory, compiled by Culpepper Tanner, was taken just a decade after the 5th Earl had inherited. It demonstrates just how much he and his wife had achieved. They bought contemporary Italian paintings, furniture, tapestries and works of art including a delicious set of eight boxwood classical figures. This all followed them back to Burghley from the continental tours they took over a period of twenty years. Not everything had to be paid for. The stunning 'rich Florentine Cabinett inlaid with stone and mother of perle, with a carv'd guilt fframe' was a gift from the Grand Duke of Tuscany. This now stands in the Heaven Room, looking like the façade of a great palazzo, the lower section supporting six Corinthian columns, and above the attic floor with a long gilt

balustrade. Where the windows and doors might have been expected, there are panels made in the ducal workshop in Florence, richly inlaid with semi-precious stones to create lively pictures of birds and flowers. These are so brilliantly achieved that it takes a moment to realize that the little bird pecking a red berry is made up of individual pieces of cut stone, thirty-nine in all, carefully chosen to achieve its graded plumage. A central door opens to reveal a mirrored theatre with a small stage that disguises the cabinet's secret drawers.

On the first floor of the west front the 5th Earl divided the sixteenth-century Long Gallery into a run of panelled rooms, which survive with their splendid (and now restored) beds. These perhaps account for some of the long lengths of fringing supplied by Dufressnoy and Lapierre at a cost of more than £1,200! Contemporary tapestries cover the walls, inset among the panelling. Passing through Paris, the earl and countess visited the Gobelins, Louis XIV's tapestry workshop, where they ordered this set of tapestries with borders containing their arms. There is a letter in the Burghley archives entreating, 'Please, my Lord, pay your bill, for you know full well I cannot sell them to anyone else', which indicates that these too were initially not paid for – the makers anxious to secure payment as the borders with the Exeter crest would make them unsaleable to other clients. In recent years this set has been taken down, restored under Lady Victoria's all-seeing eye and returned, but not before the walls had been covered with a fine cloth to stop dust coming through, and the tapestries themselves mounted with Velcro to support their weight.

The tapestries in some instances had to give way to pictures, which were arriving in their dozens. In the great state rooms on the south front, known as the George Rooms (possibly after St George, patron of the Order of the Garter, the honour given to Lord Burghley and the 1st Earl), hardly a space is left undecorated. The maestro who covered the ceilings with allegorical frescoes was Antonio Verrio, fresh from working at Windsor Castle for Charles II. He came to Burghley and stayed . . . and stayed: seemingly indispensable to his patron though often exasperating. Verrio was permanently in debt, always demanding Italian luxuries, taking his pleasure at will among the female servants, but he nevertheless created a scintillating mixture of painted architectural and classical scenes in this suite of rooms. He and his assistants tackled first the earl's Dressing Room at the south-west corner. Here his trompe l'œil ceiling shows Night giving way to Dawn with Apollo bowling across the sky in his chariot. You are amazed by his ability to create such a sense of depth and believable space on a flat ceiling. Further rich ceilings followed. In the State Bedroom, his scene shows Virtue Rewarded, whilst in the Drawing Room Cupid is reunited, and in the Dining Room the Gods are, suitably, feasting. It is in the Heaven Room where the earl and Verrio achieve their master stroke. Here not only the ceiling but the walls themselves, right down to the floor, are treated as one great painting. You stand in the centre of this space and look straight up into a mighty pedimented colonnade out of which steps Neptune, God of the Sea, with trident in hand. His

Opposite: The Heaven Room showing Antonio Verrio's illusionistic painting.

marine vehicle drawn by sea horses can be seen stationed in the water beyond. Mythological figures are rushing forward as if anxious to see for themselves what is going on on the adjacent wall. Here is a great receding hall set with classical statues: Vulcan, blacksmith's tools in hand, has laid a trap for the lovers Venus and Mars who are collapsed on a bed hung with voluminous curtains. Little do they realize that beneath lies a net which Vulcan is about to tighten around them. High up on the ceiling the Pantheon of the Gods, presided over by Jupiter and Juno in the centre, awaits the next move. Everyone is on tenterhooks.

How does Verrio achieve that sense of the Gods being among us? It is both subtle and clever. In the first instance he created his own illusionistic space with a series of great fluted Corinthian columns rising up the face of the walls that, in turn, support his painted entablature and pediment. These mask the actual point where the wall really meets the ceiling. He cleverly paints his architectural elements in shades of brown, picking up the colour of the real fitments in the room – the wooden doors and casements. Then he allows his figures to occupy his illusionary space and ours. Whole groups tumble out of the Olympian heaven as if falling into the room, whilst young Mercury, with his winged helmet and ankles, is seen flying out between the columns as if to cut across the room to get a better view. The Gods and their attendants are also life-size, giving the viewer the impression that he is part of their world just as they are part of his. This is all that Verrio wished to achieve. He was so pleased with his ability to dissolve reality that he went a step further, painting himself, bald-headed and with crayon in hand, sitting amongst his deities!

Lancelot 'Capability' Brown (1716-1783) by Sir Nathaniel Dance.

In 1700 the 5th Earl died, at Issy near Paris, apparently from a surfeit, not of art, but of fruit. His wife followed him three years later. They left behind a splendid series of rooms, a fabulous collection of paintings and works of art . . . and a mountain of debt. Verrio left before his final room was completed: his antithesis to the Heaven Room – the Hell Room. This is an extraordinary coda to his work. A vast ceiling where the ever-open jaws of hell engulf man and his works in a world ablaze with the fires of damnation. Eighty years would pass before this room was completed, and then not as intended but as a great imperial staircase inspired by the designs of Robert Adam. It was commissioned by the 5th Earl's great-grandson, Brownlow Cecil, 8th Earl of Exeter (1725–1794), who inherited Burghley in 1754 as a still unfinished house. It must have been a strange place with its large baroque room devoid of woodwork. Fortunately, the 8th Earl was very businesslike. He summoned craftsmen from London to deal with the woodworm in the Grindling Gibbons carvings and John Haynes to make a complete survey of the house and estate. Then he embarked on the completion of his ancestor's work as well as his own innovations. He was assisted by 'Capability' Brown, who was first engaged to improve the gardens and the park, and then undertook architectural work inside the house.

A succession of paintings was supplied by the earl's favourite contemporary artist, Angelica Kauffmann. She was a regular guest and a portfolio simply inscribed

Angelica remains in the house. Her splendid portrait of the 8th Earl himself, engagingly dressed in scarlet, shows a charming urbane figure at ease in his world. The painting subsequently left the collection but has been bought back recently by the trustees. He now rightly reigns over the furniture he ordered from 1767 onwards from the leading London firm Mayhew & Ince. Being an eighteenth-century connoisseur he naturally went on the Grand Tour, leaving England soon after the Seven Years War was concluded in 1763 and returning two years later. In Italy he showed himself to be a discerning patron, acquiring the rich marble and porphyry fireplace to a design by Piranesi, now in the State Bedroom, and a series of Old Master paintings. Perhaps the most beautiful of these is Jacopo Bassano's *Adoration of the Magi*, which hangs in the Red Drawing Room flanked by two Veroneses he also bought. The *Adoration* shows the Virgin in profile to the left, beneath a broken column, holding the infant Christ. Leaning over her is St Joseph, and at her feet a curled-up dog who is trying to get some sleep – a typical Bassano touch. In the centre the three magi bend forward with their gifts, as costly as their raiment, and to the right the attendants noisily await their masters. A great grey horse is bending its neck, full of implied movement, whilst a young man has encouraged another dog to leap up to be patted. It is a rich Venetian confection propelling the biblical story into contemporary world, complete with a delicious north Italian landscape blending into the blue alpine mountains behind.

There are a number of ways to explore Burghley. One of the most unusual is to come to it underground, and that is exactly what happens if you go down to the cellars. Simon Leatham led the way as we went from one cavernous corridor to another, passing all the way along the south front. You are eventually brought to a subterranean hall, the light percolating in through leaded panes. Great stone sinks built into the walls survive from the sixteenth and seventeenth centuries; far too heavy to lug up the ramp that leads to the back courts. Down here also lies the wine cellar. When Simon and Lady Victoria first came to Burghley these looked as abundant as the teeming cupboards upstairs, but as the bottles were sorted each in turn was found to be empty!

Another way to arrive is by the present main entrance on the north front. It was here that Queen Victoria's carriage drew up in 1844 when she came to visit Prince Albert's Groom of the Stole, and later her Lord Chamberlain, Brownlow, 2nd Marquess of Exeter (1795–1867), and his rather pious marchioness. A small painting by Barraud shows Queen Victoria and Prince Albert alighting, about to enter through the golden gates. Her Majesty was making a progress through the country and, as Lord Lieutenant, Lord Exeter had been accompanying her. Now he had the opportunity to show her his house and lavish preparations had been made, not least in the State Bedroom where the Regency bed supplied by Newton & Fell to the Marquess's father was teased into something more dazzling. Its great independent canopy was scrapped and in its place a new domed tester was made, surmounted by a pair of cooing doves nestling in a wreath. The underside of the dome was richly quilted, with the initials of the queen and her consort picked out in gold. As if to confirm the royal occupancy the words *Victoria Regina* are also to be found on its top and the gilded royal arms pop up above the headboard. All the woodwork, originally a rich mahogany, was also gilded and the red-striped upholstery was trimmed out with gold thread, braids and tassels. Opposite, the sixteenth-century windows were afforded similar treatment, topped by two pale cherubs holding aloft a gilded crown which almost reaches the ceiling. A contemporary watercolour depicts the banquet given in the Great Hall. The queen sat next to her host, near the fireplace, surrounded by guests in their finery, and served by gentlemen in livery with spotless white breeches.

But all did not quite go to plan. The Prince Consort had agreed to be sponsor to the Exeters' latest child, appropriately named Victoria. Another print shows the ceremony taking place in the private chapel on the first floor at Burghley. Unfortunately the Bishop of Peterborough, who was conducting the service, was unnerved by the grandeur of the occasion. He misguidedly took a little sherry to calm his nerves, and then discovered he had forgotten his spectacles. He commenced the proceedings only to discover that neither the baby nor the queen had arrived. Eventually, however, everything was sorted out and the baby received her royal name. The party relaxed a little and went out onto the south lawn to plant a commemorative tree. But it was quite a mistake to give the diminutive queen such a large and heavy spade to carry out this task and she staggered

around making a number of unconvincing stabs at the soil. She turned to her worried host to ask for a lighter tool. Fortunately he had the presence of mind to go to his children's sandpit and collect a humble little turned wood spade. It did the trick. The tree was planted and the spade put on display to commemorate a not wholly happy royal visit.

Visitors today see much more of the house and collection than Queen Victoria did. It has been one of the characteristics of Simon and Lady Victoria's tenure that restoration has been carried out in tandem with new projects. As Simon says, up to twenty independent schemes can be taking place in any year. They both admit it is difficult to know when to stop but now they think it is time to leave Burghley and let the next generation take up the challenge. Of course, the plans they have set in motion will continue after their departure: a new exhibition hall will be going up in the stable block and a garden, inspired by those familiar to Lord Burghley, will be planted in the park.

The banquet for Queen Victoria held in the Great Hall in 1844 by Henry Bryant Ziegler.

Dalmeny House, West Lothian

The seat of the Earls of Rosebery and Midlothian

Previous spread: *Dalmeny from across the park.*

Sometimes you discover a great building rather obliquely. This was certainly the case with Dalmeny. My first impressions were not glimpsing it from the Firth of Forth, but rather it grew in my mind through casual comments caught far away in the Vale of Aylesbury. It was here in Buckinghamshire, at the family's great inherited house of Mentmore, that I first met Neil and Deirdre Primrose in the mid 1970s when they had fairly recently become the new Earl and Countess of Rosebery. Whilst trying to make sense of their inheritance and deciding on the family's future, it was clear that their paramount objective was to preserve and enhance Dalmeny, even if it meant that Mentmore would have to be sold. It all seemed slightly puzzling. Mentmore was such a great house, a dazzling Victorian *tour de force* and Paxton's architectural masterpiece. It was approached from a private railway station, up a double avenue of majestic Wellingtonias, and was situated on a carefully selected platform on the Chilterns with stunning views. It was also layered with fabulous works of art – trophies of craftsmanship from all over Europe prompting the author Henry James to liken this Rothschild palace to the houses of the Medici. It was difficult to imagine the family's Scottish house being able to hold up a candle to this . . . indeed, I was incredulous almost to the point of disbelief: surely the Rosebery family were simply putting on a brave face.

Well, you live and learn. Some months later, after the dust had settled on the Mentmore sale, I was in Edinburgh and drove out to see the Dalmeny estate, which lies between the city's western boundaries and the famous Firth of Forth railway bridge at South Queensferry. The drive to the house drops down from the main road following the contours of the hills, passing through fine old woods and fields. Then at one glorious moment the view opens up to a panorama incorporating a huge inland estuary littered with tiny islands, an ancient castle built right on the water's edge, and a Gothic mansion looking like an architect's model in its pristine purity, all surrounded by groves of trees and grassy sward. The scudding clouds meant that the whole view continually shifted and changed, with the noise of the sea birds and the lapping of the waves giving it an unexpected energy. Any disbelief I had fell away. I could quite see why Neil and Deirdre knew that there was really no contest between Dalmeny and Mentmore. Many houses are beautifully set in their estates but few have such magical natural surroundings. There is also poignancy in the view, edged on one side by the great city of Edinburgh and on the other by the busy Forth Bridge, creating a pleasant tension between the ancient, permanent qualities of the estate and the more transient day-to-day activities beyond.

Continuing down the drive through a series of hairpin bends, passing the Home Farm, you emerge at the end of a large stretch of grass, subtly planted with specimen trees and copses, which has doubled as the estate golf course since the middle of the last century. The main house becomes clearer from here and the sprinkling of Gothic turrets glimpsed from above turn out to be ornamental chimney stacks built of Coade stone. The building is wholly successful, a very early essay in the Gothic Revival: one that would in due course spawn many offspring in the works of Burns and Bryce. Its style is freely adapted late Gothic, with steep gables, oriel windows and quatrefoil panels. It is built of a hard-wearing local stone into which grooves have been drilled to give it greater character; and enlivened by panels of heraldic ornaments, again purpose-made at the Coade factory in London and shipped to Scotland. It looks as if it was all carefully thought through: and it was.

Among the family papers, now meticulously catalogued by the Roseberys' second daughter, Lady Jane Kaplan, are the architectural designs for the house. These reveal a prolonged gestation period covering almost fifty years and involving two generations of Primroses; the 3rd and 4th Earls. When Neil Primrose, 3rd Earl of Rosebery (1728–1814), inherited in 1755 the family were still living in Barnbougle Castle, the ancient fortification at the water's edge which had originally been acquired by his great-grandfather, Archibald Primrose (1616–1679), in 1662. It had a commanding position overseeing the shipping in the Firth of Forth and over the years had also become the centre of a growing landed estate. Archibald laid the foundation of the family fortune. He inherited his father's position as clerk to the Scottish Privy Council but this adherence to the Stuart dynasty was to cost him dear. He was captured following the battle of Philiphaugh in 1645 and found guilty of treason, but somehow managed to talk his way out of prison the following year. Charles I knighted him after the battle of Worcester; Charles II made him a baronet in 1651. His estates, though, were sequestrated and it was only at the Restoration in 1660 that his fortune, in all senses, improved. He was made Lord Register of Scotland that year, a post he was to keep for sixteen years, Lord of the Sessions and, eventually, Lord Chief Justice of Scotland. He thus became a very powerful and influential figure in the government, enabling him to build up estates of which Dalmeny was the most valuable.

Sir Archibald's eldest son by his adroit second marriage to Agnes Gray, the widow of Sir James Dundas, was also called Archibald (1664–1723). He became Member of Parliament for Edinburgh and in London was a gentleman of the bedchamber to Prince George of Denmark, consort of Queen Anne. Not surprisingly, this influential politician and courtier was made a Commissioner for the Union of the Kingdoms of England and Scotland and, to ensure his support, he was elevated to a viscountcy in 1700 and to an earldom in 1703. This shift in the family's position can be sensed when comparing the portraits of father and son. Sir Archibald, painted by the Edinburgh artist David Scougal, looks the wily lawyer he undoubtedly was, whereas Sir Godfrey Kneller produced a polished portrait of an equally polished 1st Earl. In the next generation his son James, 2nd Earl of Rosebery (1680–1755), should have consolidated the family's position at the centre of Anglo-Scottish affairs when he married Lady Mary Campbell, sister of the country's leading politician, John, 4th Duke of Argyll. But all families can throw up a black sheep, and he was one. He deserted his wife for the favours of a laundry maid and was subsequently imprisoned for riot and debt. The estates were put in the hands of trustees; the sole advantage of this unfortunate situation was that it kept the family out of the Jacobite controversies.

Happily for the family, Neil Primrose, 3rd Earl of Rosebery (1728–1814), who inherited in 1755, was made of sterner stuff. His earlier career as a London merchant stood him and the estate in good stead. He reorganized the farms, enclosing the land, and paid off the debts that had encumbered the family for nearly twenty years. His marriage in 1764 to the heiress Susan Ward further lined the coffers, and consideration was given to building a new house, one more convenient than Barnbougle Castle. There was clearly architectural competition from his neighbours, such as the Hopes who had erected a baroque palace at Hopetoun, just a few miles up the Firth of Forth. However, it was not until after the early death of his wife that he turned to Scotland's most famous architect, Robert Adam. In 1774 Adam produced ground plans and elevations for a building that hovers between the Emperor Diocletian's palace at Split on the Adriatic coast and Gormenghast, complete with an oval harbour, presumably to receive the earl's boat when he made his way up the Firth from Edinburgh. One senses that the plans frightened the client; they were too outrageous, too disruptive and, above all, too expensive – the earl was famously careful with his money.

The following years saw a second marriage, to Mary Vincent, followed by a period of domestic felicity with a growing brood of children. These times are caught in the enchanting conversation piece of the whole family painted by a

local artist, Alexander Nasmyth, in 1788. Here the 3rd Earl stands with a hat firmly perched on his head (to disguise his encroaching baldness) and holding the hand of his son and heir. To the left stands his wife, also wearing a smart hat, next to her eldest daughter and with the younger children gathered around a rose bush. For all its charm the painting points up the lack of architectural distinction of Barnbougle. This white harled building was in essence a large tower with a winding staircase leading from one floor to another, and an assortment of low buildings attached in a rather haphazard manner. It had been occasionally updated but it was very inconvenient. The present earl tells the story that, one night after dinner, his predecessor was passing through the lower corridor when not only did the wind blow out his sole candle but he then was drenched by an unusually high wave crashing in through the window. The 3rd Earl's response to such misfortune in his later years was simply to say that what was good enough for his grandfather was good enough for him!

As time passed the earl grew richer, aided in part by the sale of stone from his quarries to build the growing New Town in Edinburgh. He also grew older, but that did nothing to diminish his personal vanity. As the present Lady Rosebery recalls, he had three wigs – one short, one medium and one long. He would wear

them in turn and when he judged it time he would announce that he was going to visit Edinburgh to visit his barber. Off in the carriage he would go, returning some hours later wearing the short wig – and woe betide anyone who made a less than supportive comment! Today the great full-length portrait of the earl by Sir Henry Raeburn, resplendent in his robes as a Knight of the Thistle, dominates the dining room, staring down on the company having clearly just had a 'haircut'. His sweet wife, Susan, had to be content with a half-length portrait by George Romney, painted when they were in London – she must have attended the artist's studio up on Hampstead Hill. The painting of her mother, Lady Vincent, in contrast, is a wonder of German-Italian eighteenth-century art. The sitter was painted in a dazzling pink gown holding a mask, caught just before leaving for a ball. The artist, Mengs, one of the prime movers of the neoclassical movement, is not normally given to such successful excess. You feel that Lady Vincent was quite a character. I love the way she hangs adjacent to her son-in-law who looks as if he cannot decide how he is going to deal with her.

It eventually fell to the earl's son, her grandson, to make the decisive move and finally commission a new house. Lord Archibald John Primrose was born in 1783 and after Eton went to Cambridge, where he fell in with a group of young dilettantes keen on architecture, archaeology and the arts. Here was a young man impatient with his father's procrastination, and plans first by William Atkinson and then by William Wilkins began to arrive for a smart classical building but again nothing was built. In 1814 two events occurred that suddenly removed all impediments; Lord Archibald's father died and his wife, Harriet Bouverie, bolted – the subsequent divorce in the House of Lords producing a prodigious financial settlement for the innocent young earl. With only a momentary hesitation, when he switched from classical to Gothic, the earl invited Wilkins to build him a new house. As these plans became a reality, the idea of building on a high bluff was abandoned, for as Deirdre Rosebery averts, the gradient would have crippled the horses. (She should know, as her early life was gallantly spent entertaining endless Pony Club camps at Dalmeny, and her eldest and youngest daughters are keen equestriennes.)

The exterior of the house today is almost exactly as William Wilkins intended. His brand of Gothic derives from his studies of East Barsham Manor in Norfolk and from his earlier work, including the hall and great screen at King's College Cambridge. However, the interior of the house did pass through some significant changes. These are well known to the current earl, who has often had recourse to the original plans when dealing with rewiring, replumbing, indeed almost re-everything during the last thirty years. The building work lasted from 1814 to 1817 and inside there is a pleasing balance between Gothic, for the great Staircase Hall and main corridor, and classical, for the adjacent enfilade of state rooms.

The Staircase Hall rises up three storeys and is top-lit by lancet windows. The hammer-beam ceiling is a nice fudge: no massive beams here, rather wood and plaster carefully grained to look like the real thing. The blank Gothic niches were not all intended as ornamental. The one on the first rise of the staircase was to have been a doorcase matching that on the other side but the idea of an imperial staircase bifurcating at the centre point was abandoned, leaving the potential doorcase stranded halfway up the wall. (Wilkins managed to get another client, Lord Falmouth, to retain the imperial staircase when he came to build another 'Dalmeny' at Tregothnan a decade later. He must have felt he could get away with a near copy as this second house, in the south of Cornwall, could hardly have been further away.) The Gothic corridor runs at right angles off the Staircase Hall, replete with Gothic arches, a ribbed ceiling and strongly coloured stained-glass windows. These were an inspired purchase by the 4th Earl, as not only are they wonderful sixteenth-century glass in their own right but they also solved the problem of getting light into this area without seeing the internal courtyard beyond. It is in this corridor that some of the 4th Earl's pictures now hang, including an early portrait of Edward VI.

The portrait of his cousin once removed, James VI of Scotland and I of England, was acquired later, from the Duke of Hamilton's collection at Hamilton Palace (a sale occasioned in part by the palace collapsing into a mine shaft). It shows the monarch painted by his court artist John de Critz, dressed to the nines. Not the least resplendent are the pearls coursing over the whole of his doublet and hose, seeming to act as expensive stitching, while his hat contains an enormous jewelled cockade comprising the famous 'Three Brothers', a trio of very large diamonds – some of the largest stones in the old English crown jewels – set against black foil. Sadly these stones now have pride of place in the Louvre, having been pawned by the king's daughter-in-law, Henrietta Maria, to Cardinal Mazarin for much-needed funds to support her husband Charles I; from the Cardinal they passed to the French Crown. Beneath this portrait lies another historic relic: an enormous bladed weapon which Neil Rosebery asserts is a covenanter's execution sword (but if so, why the two blades?). This fiendish object retains all its lengthy sharpness albeit safely ensconced in a decorated wooden frame.

At the end of the Gothic corridor lies the Dining Room, which retains its late Regency flavour. It is thickly hung with eighteenth- and nineteenth-century portraits: those of the family interspersed with contemporary historical figures

such as Reynolds' perceptive portrait of Edward Gibbons, author of *The Decline and Fall of the Roman Empire*. The sitter confessed himself not to be handsome, but Reynolds overcomes this by showing him in half-profile. The white marble busts which enliven the corners of this noble room include likenesses of Lord Chesterfield and Lord Rockingham, the latter looking down his remarkably elegant nose. The rich mahogany furniture is also largely contemporary with the room, some supplied by the excellent Edinburgh makers Trotters. Adjacent lies the former Billiard Room, and beyond the Drawing Room and Library.

In the opposite direction from the Staircase Hall runs a shorter corridor off which lie the private apartments for the 4th Earl and his new countess. He married as his second wife Lady Anne Anson, the sister of the 1st Earl of Lichfield from Shugborough in Staffordshire, in 1819. The intimate rooms found there lead into a private walled garden where the Roseberys would have been joined by their children: Archibald, Lord Dalmeny, his brother and sister Bouverie and

Left: *Archibald Philip, 5th Earl of Rosebery (1847–1929), by Sir John Everett Millais P.R.A.*

Opposite: *Edward Gibbon (1737–1794), author of* The Decline and Fall of the Roman Empire *by Sir Joshua Reynolds P.R.A.*

Harriet, and their new half-sisters, Anne and Louisa. The 4th Earl and his countess were to live long lives – so long that they outlived their heir Lord Dalmeny, whose portrait by Sir Francis Grant hangs high up in the Staircase Hall. A serious young man who entered political life and became a Lord of the Admiralty, he was propelled into activity by his redoubtable wife, Lady Wilhelmina Stanhope, the only daughter of Lord Stanhope. He was a tireless proponent of physical exercise, an early jogger, who sadly succumbed to his enthusiasm by expiring on a water closet at Dalmeny having run all the way to the house from Edinburgh.

Another portrait in the hall depicts his son, the 4th Earl's grandson and eventual heir, Archibald Philip, who was born in 1848 and was only three when his father died. He was largely brought up by his mother and her family, the Stanhopes,

with his step-father, the Duke of Cleveland. Although probably apocryphal, his contemporaries felt that this precocious youth had three ambitions in life – to marry an heiress, to win the Derby and to be prime minister. If this were the case he certainly lived up to expectations. The portrait by Sir John Everett Millais, and the delicate white marble bust by Boehm that stands nearby, show a young man of ambition, slightly fastidious in his dress but with an engaging open smile. He was popular and bright and his family connections and extensive friendships soon placed him at the centre of society. In 1878, at the age of 31, he surprised some and delighted others when he married Hannah de Rothschild, the only daughter and heir to Baron Mayer Amschel de Rothschild. There were comments in the Rothschild family about seepage of the family fortune and tittle-tattle in the papers about an English earl marrying outside the 'pale'. But it was nothing. Theirs was a happy marriage, sustained by their love for each other, an intelligent cultivated attitude to life, and mutual enjoyment of their wealth and position. Within a relatively short space of time Dalmeny became but one of a series of family houses which included Mentmore, a large town house in Berkeley Square, the Durdans down at Epsom for the racing, and, in due course and perhaps most surprising, the Villa Rosebery outside Naples.

The great Rothschild collection of continental paintings, furniture and works of art assembled at Mentmore by the baron formed the background to Hannah's taste, and she certainly infected her husband with an enthusiasm for buying yet more. The couple celebrated their marriage by acquiring two of Turner's masterpieces, *Rome from Mount Aventine* and *Rome in Modern Times* (now on long-term loan to the National Gallery of Scotland). This was but a foretaste to the acquisition of books, silver, old master paintings, furniture and works of art. There was a significant difference between the Rothschild taste and that of the 5th Earl of Rosebery. He was often as fascinated by the historical associations of a work of art as by its aesthetic qualities. His collection of Scottish furniture is now displayed in the Gothic corridor, his portraits of statesmen in the Dining Room, and his views of eighteenth-century London hang high up in the Staircase Hall. Above all, works of art associated with the life of the Emperor Napoleon, now in the old Billiard Room (fittingly now re-christened the Napoleon Room) attest to this aspect of the earl's taste.

Opposite: *The entrance front of Mentmore in Buckinghamshire, built for Baron Meyer de Rothschild, by H. W. Brewer.*

Left: *Napoleon after the Battle of Lodi by Andrea Appiani, 1796.*

Although published in 1922, Rosebery's book, *Napoleon: The Last Phase*, was the outcome of years of studying the life of this French colossus. Its physical embodiment today is the collection of Napoleana that lies at the heart of Dalmeny, the greatest outside France. Here are found the portraits by Lefebvre of the Emperor's immediate family alongside two ravishing portraits of Napoleon himself, both by Andrea Appiani, showing how rapid was his development from military commander to a ruler with imperial ambitions. The first shows him as a slender figure, after the battle of Lodi in 1796 where he had brilliantly outwitted and then routed the Austrian forces, leaving the north of Italy his for the taking. The Angel of Victory stands beside the youthful conqueror recording his achievements. The second painting, only a decade later, shows a much more confident image. Gone is the young bashful man, replaced by one with almost overwhelming confidence. The bulkier figure is now resplendent in a sumptuous uniform, his newly invented Order, the Légion d'Honneur, catching the light as it hangs proudly on his puffed-out chest. He is now emperor and King of Italy. His gloved hand rests firmly on his newly acquired crown.

These contrasts are to be caught elsewhere in the room. The simple mahogany throne designed by Jacob, used by Napoleon when consul, looks positively humble when compared to his washstand (formerly at Malmaison). This is

Opposite: *Napoleon as King of Italy by Andrea Appiani, painted after his coronation in Milan in 1806.*

Above: *Napoleon's deathbed with the emperor surrounded by members of his household by Baron Steuben.*

ornamented with his own profile portrait, surrounded by his symbol of the busy bee. The room also has relics from the end of his life. The painting by the young Charles Eastlake, who was eventually to become Keeper of the National Gallery in London, shows the emperor on *The Bellerophon* in Torquay Bay standing proud but slightly confused prior to his voyage in the *Northumberland* (a model of which stands in this room) to his exile in St Helena. From that island comes the modest table and chairs from his study, designed by George Bullock, the white painted screens which he had erected in this house, Longwood, to stop the impertinent gaze of the young officers, and the scene of his deathbed by Baron Steuben. These are relics of the utmost importance and, not surprisingly, Dalmeny is a place of pilgrimage for Napoleonophiles. The deathbed scene is a case in point. Arguments continue as to why the emperor died – was it the arsenic in the

wallpaper? Was it just a poor diet? Steuben's painting is thought to be the most accurate depiction of his last moments, based on the first-hand description of the scene surrounded by his own staff and members of the English garrison. Rosebery's interest in Napoleon led in turn to his adversaries and close to the painting stands the Duke of Wellington's campaign chair, infinitely grander than the emperor's Bullock furniture. This is an all-singing, all-dancing object with a cushioned pull-out stool and collapsible, adjustable writing stand extending from the arm. Everything a general might need on campaign (provided he has the people to carry it!).

The furniture and works of art in the adjacent drawing room, although also French, speak of another world altogether. When Mentmore was sold it was decided to bring its grandest treasures north. Fortunately, the drawing room had over the years been surrendered to two grand pianos, the pride of Neil's mother Eva, Countess of Rosebery, who was a very accomplished musician and co-founder

Opposite: *The Napoleon Room showing the Duke of Wellington's campaign chair and Napoleon's desk and screen from St Helena.*

Left: *A Beauvais tapestry designed in 1740 by Francois Boucher in the Chinese taste. Part of the set which hangs in the Drawing Room.*

of the Edinburgh Festival. She and her instruments departed for Newmarket and this, the largest of the state rooms, was ready and waiting. It did not have to wait long for the great Savonniery carpet to be laid, the chinoiserie tapestries designed by François Boucher to be hung (interspersed with paintings by Greuze and his school) and furniture of outstanding quality to be introduced. The selection and arrangement were made by Deirdre Rosebery who, by her own admission, had been on a steep learning curve since the Mentmore decision had been taken. With great assurance she created a harmonious room from objects that in a museum would be treated with such reverence that they would be singled out for individual treatment. There is also wit. I love the way the somewhat aloof busts of Louis XVI and his wife Marie Antoinette stand on the great desk belonging to the Ministère de Finance, Monsieur Jacques Necker – supported, literally and metaphysically, by the financial machinery of late-eighteenth-century France.

Sadly for Necker, the problems proved intractable and in the wake of the French Revolution the 'busts' would lose their heads courtesy of the guillotine. The desk by Jean-François Leleu, a lasting symbol of the Ancien Régime, is both magnificent and huge: a spectacular piece of French neoclassical furniture in gleaming mahogany enriched by ormolu decoration. When closed, all is compact and safe, as the cylindrical lid emerges from deep within and pulls forward to cover the desk top. When opened, it reveals a surface large enough to cope with reams of papers. At the sides are two separate pull-out surfaces used by Necker's secretaries – he had the ability, and need, to dictate to two of them simultaneously.

The remarkable ability of French and German designers to create stunning furniture that is both practical and beautiful is replicated throughout the room. From a decade earlier is the table by David Roentgen. What appears at first sight to be an elegant if simple piece, albeit with a stunning top of inlaid and coloured woods depicting an architect at work, is in fact a jack-in-a-box of tricks. Deirdre, I know, loves to show this off – displaying the designer's brilliance and allowing her to act as the magician. One pull here, one turn there and 'hey presto!', the piece reveals itself as a writing table replete with endless compartments for all that a man of business might require. No wonder Roentgen is considered to be one of the greatest furniture designers ever. Sidling back in time a little further, you are confronted with the rococo desk created by Bernard van Reisenberghe (B.V.R.B.) for Louis XV's eldest son, the Dauphin. Here floral inlay runs all over the piece, which itself curves in and out. It is almost impossible to imagine how you construct something out of wood that writhes so elegantly. Neil and

Left: *Ingenious 18th-century French gaming machine, designed and made by Gallonde in Paris, 1739.*

Deirdre know, as when the piece came up from Mentmore its veneers were lifting, especially along the back where it had been exposed to too much sunlight. This was rectified but in the process everyone learned that such pieces are not only brilliantly constructed but are also very fragile. The curtains are now kept tightly drawn in the Drawing Room.

One smaller piece, a real rich-man's toy, is the gaming machine made in Paris in 1739 by Gallonde. No other example is known, which is surprising as it is such fun, but I imagine the cost even then was off-putting. A curvaceous ornate mounted box, again inlaid with flowers, contains a winding mechanism which spins three dice. When the whirring is over, the dice gently rise to the surface, like champagne bubbles, revealing the numbers through a glass. What an easy way to make (or probably lose!) a fortune. So much easier than throwing dice across a table and having to reach for the one that rolls on the floor. The ingenuity of France is seen everywhere in this room, from the beautiful pink and green ground Sèvres *eccuelles* (for refreshing your glasses in ice water) to the poignant model of Marie Antoinette's dog sitting on his cushion. The queen even managed to smuggle this memento into the Conciergerie Prison – it survived; she did not. This is a room which reveals the remarkable innovative taste of Baron Mayer de Rothschild, collecting in the middle of the nineteenth century, and the knowledge and appreciation of his descendants in Scotland today.

This sense of continuity and change is a hallmark of the house and family. The Regency Gothic mansion has accommodated the treasures from Mentmore and the family have equally adapted the house to suit their own needs. The old private apartments, last used by Neil's parents, are now full of further treasures from the family's other houses. The present family have created their own private rooms upstairs. Here they live in former bedrooms and nurseries running, as downstairs, off a central corridor. As Neil is quick to point out, he is following the practice of his forebears. They too knew that there was no financial sense in lighting and heating the whole house every day if no one was going to use the state rooms. Neil is the descendant of a family of canny Scots. Deirdre, who grew up near the coast in East Anglia, is equally happy with the arrangement. Being on the first floor, looking out of Wilkins' generous windows, means that you enjoy the ever-changing view. The park, the hills and the Firth of Forth – one of many telling factors that meant the family were happy to relinquish Buckinghamshire for the sheer pleasures of their ancient seat in Scotland. As if to underline this point, when Carlos Sanchez painted the family, they asked him to use Dalmeny's shoreline as a background, echoing Nasmyth's portrait of 200 years previously. It depicts a family who have loved, nurtured and improved this part of Scotland since the early 1660s.

Deene Park,
Northamptonshire

The seat of the Brudenell Family

Previous spread: *Deene Park from across the lake.*

Opposite: *The North Entrance Front showing the 17th-century façade.*

Appearances can be deceptive. Standing in front of the main entrance to Deene Park, you might easily think you have arrived at a fine seventeenth-century house. On the first floor is a regular march of five large casement windows, suggesting a grand chamber or long gallery. This is emphasized by both the smallness of the windows on the ground floor, and the importance of the great chimneys, rising like rockets into the sky. Surely Deene must be a Carolean house, built by a family who had done well during the time of the Civil War. But this would be conjecture, and all of it mistaken. Deene does not give up its history that easily, nor reveal its full architectural complexity from a single vantage point.

There has been a house here since medieval times, yet this has been so altered and added to that its early appearance has simply vanished. If that was not enough to confuse, walls have been erected only to come down again, fireplaces introduced here have moved there, wings have stretched out only to be later curtailed and whole façades have been built, dismantled and built once again. It is a place where you need to stand still and stare to let Deene slowly unveil its complex past. Even the main entrance frontage can reveal a little more. Certainly the façade is seventeenth century in date but the main door is not; its deep-fielded panels, now worn and patched, must date from a century later. And the little cast-iron boot scraper, with its morsel of classical decoration, surely dates from the 1820s. Clearly this is a house that has been growing and changing its character over many years, altered and improved by generations of Brudenells.

The family came to this part of Northamptonshire when Sir Robert Brudenell (1461–1531) acquired the Manor of Deene in 1514 from the Litton family. He was born in Amersham in Buckinghamshire, the second son of Edmund Brudenell. He made his way in life through the law: he was said to have spent some time

at King's College Cambridge; more certainly he entered the Inner Temple in London in 1480. During the next twenty years he rose rapidly in his profession, becoming a leading lawyer in the first half of Henry VII's reign. In 1504 he was made one of the king's sergeants, a judge of the King's Bench just three years later, and from 1520 to 1530 he was Chief Justice of the Common Pleas. The law was, and is, a lucrative business. His substantial fortune was further increased by his first marriage, in 1495, to Margaret Entwistle, heiress to her father's estate at Stanton Wyville in Leicestershire. Yet further property was acquired in Rutland, Buckinghamshire and Lincolnshire, and by the time of his death Sir Robert was a wealthy man. Whilst he may not have lived much at Deene, he arranged that he should be buried there. Today, just as he directed in his will, he lies between his first and second wives, his full-length figure in official robes with his Chief Justice's double-S collar sculpted around his neck. No other contemporary portrait has survived but his descendants in the late seventeenth century remedied this deficiency, commissioning a great full-length image of him, resplendent

in rich red judicial robes. This portrait by Jean Baptiste Gaspars now hangs in pride of place in the Great Hall built by his grandson.

A glimpse of the house Sir Robert Brudenell acquired is just discernible in the Inner Courtyard. Entering through the eighteenth-century panelled front entrance and passing under an arch, you find yourself in the courtyard, of the type most familiar in the collegiate buildings at Oxford and Cambridge. On the east side is the much altered range of his building, now with a run of seventeenth-century windows interrupted by a large oriel window, possibly from his Great Hall. The early architectural development of the house is referred to in a painted inscription on another wall which reads 'He [Sir Robert] Built in the First Place the Northern Building. The Southern Thomas [his son, Sir Thomas] a Pious and Learned man Built. The Third, Higher than the Rest, was built at the Expense of Edmund [his grandson, Sir Edmund]'. The first phase on the northern side has been swept away by subsequent work, but an arch in the southern range adjacent to the Great Hall survives, still bearing the arms of Sir Thomas and his wife, embellished with spandrels. The later sixteenth-century buildings are certainly the work of Sir Edmund.

Sir Edmund (1521–1585) inherited Deene in 1549, and records show that building work was underway within five years. Although only in his twenties, he was clearly responding to his architecturally competitive neighbours. This part of north Northamptonshire, between the market towns of Stamford, Oundle and Corby, is today a peaceful rural retreat. The gently undulating countryside, populated by small villages with spired churches standing amidst cottages and farms, does not resound often with the noise of great building works. It was a different story in the sixteenth century. Northamptonshire was the place to live, and to show off your wealth and sophistication. The county provided a rich source of stone; vibrant ironstone to the south and paler Collyweston stone in the north-east. It was also rich in potential sites; in 1590 Norden compiled his list of 'salutarie and profitable seates' and included fifty-nine in this small part of the country. The virtues of the area were further endorsed by the cartographer John Speed, who included twenty-seven parks in his map printed in 1610, an increase from the twenty listed by Christopher Saxton thirty years previously. Among these new neighbours were the Montagus at Boughton, the FitzWilliams at Milton and the Cecils at Burghley. No wonder William Camden noted that the county was 'passing well furnish'd with noblemen's and gentlemen's houses'.

Little is known of Sir Edmund's early foray into building. It is probable that the highly elaborate triple-banked block (now full of blind windows and applied to the east front) may date from the mid 1500s, moved to its current position later. If this is the case, it reveals a level of architectural panache that would hopefully have appealed to Elizabeth I, who visited Deene in the summer of 1566. Fortunately, much more is known of Sir Edmund's second phase of building work; and much more remains. In 1571 Sir Edmund confided in his diary that he 'laid the foundation of my hall at Deene', and that building still dominates the south side of the courtyard. This is a splendid affair, entered by way of a classical, Italianate double-height porch – an attractive counterweight to the large oriel window. In the upper half, a tripartite window is caught between two Corinthian pilasters, each decorated with a herringbone pattern, whilst the door beneath is flanked by Ionic pilasters carved with even more elaborate decoration. The frieze above the door is beautifully worked, with a design of birds, tendrils, putti and mermaids who support the arms of Brudenell and his wife, Agnes Bussy. The original hall screen was removed some time after 1746, so now you are afforded an uninterrupted view as you enter the room and turn eastwards. The floor, set with square flags, leads the eye towards the far end. Here the wall is half covered with particularly fine panelling incorporating ribbed pilasters and surmounted by a sumptuous centrepiece containing a carved family armorial, supported on either side by half-naked herms. The elaborate fireplace on the south wall replaced a Victorian horror. It may well have originated here, being dated 1571, but latterly stood in the Billiard Room. Like the porch, it is of beautifully articulated stone, its design surely influenced by French and Italian architectural books of the period. The whole hall, is flooded with light from a succession of windows which leaves only the great chestnut roof, a complex design of hammer beams alternating with collared trusses, in partial obscurity.

This noble room has suffered over the years from well-meant but inappropriate alterations. The slow process of bringing it back to its original form was started in the twentieth century by George Brudenell, father of Edmund, the current owner. He removed the panelling and more recently the walls have been painted a harmonious cream and the furniture rearranged so that the great sixteenth-century table can be laid for tea in the winter, guests having to balance themselves on the long benches. Oak furniture has been reintroduced, including a pair of antiquarian sofas that extend invitingly on either side of the fireplace.

The gentle progression of Sir Edmund's building programme, culminating in this spectacular Great Hall, might suggest an easy life. In some respects this is true – though twice high sheriff of Northampton and knighted by the queen at Charlecote in 1565, he never stood for Parliament nor sought any office at court. He seems to have been content to build up his estates, improve the house and beyond that to interest himself in genealogy – a continuing passion in the Brudenell family. It comes, then, as a surprise to discover, through contemporary documents, that his peace was rocked by continuous quarrels with his wife Agnes. She seemed to have all the qualities he would have looked for – an ancient pedigree and oodles of money – but these were insufficient to calm the matrimonial waters, which were stilled only by her death in 1583. Sir Edmund himself died two years later to be succeeded by his two younger brothers. Eventually, in 1606, Deene passed to the next generation in the person of Edmund's nephew, Thomas.

Thomas Brudenell (1578–1663) was to own the estate for more than fifty years. On paper his life would appear to have been a seamless success: ennobled as Lord Brudenell of Stanton Wyville by Charles I in 1628 and elevated to the Earldom of Cardigan by Charles II in 1661. However, his portrait, painted by John Michael Wright in 1658, suggests a more complex story. He stands surprisingly upright for a man in his seventies, slightly supporting himself with his left hand on the back of a chair. His face is careworn, surrounded by lank grey hair, yet his stare is honest and penetrating. The passing of his days is reflected by the sunset shown behind him, but his grip on life remains tight, his hand shown close to the hilt of his sword and with a firm hold on his gloves. This is the portrait of a man who has weathered the vicissitudes of life in England during the first half of the seventeenth century, holding true to himself and his faith.

The son of Robert Brudenell and Catherine Taylard, Thomas was brought up in the Catholic faith of her family. This was reinforced by his marriage in 1605 to Mary Tresham, whose father was the most prominent recusant in this part of the country and whose brother was to be executed for his involvement in the Gunpowder Plot. Like his father-in-law, Thomas Brudenell had a deep interest in scholarship, antiquarianism and architecture. In Tresham's case, this saw

expression in his buildings at Rothwell, Rushton with its triangular lodge dedicated to the Holy Trinity, and Lyveden New Build. Brudenell's buildings were of an equally high quality. The tower to the north-east of the house was raised by him and is peppered in the Tresham manner with family armorials. Similarly the large windows in his uncle's Great Hall were filled with stained glass depicting the armorial achievements of both the Brudenells and the Treshams (these were blown out during the Second World War but have been restored by the current owners, Edmund and his wife Marion). In the Tapestry Room Thomas's work may be found in pristine condition. Entering this room on the first floor of the east wing, you cannot help but stare at the sheer mastery of his plaster ceiling: a series of extravagant pendant bosses, contained in rippling circles of plaster alternated with wide flattened roses. The spaces between are set with geometric patterns decorated with vines, whilst emblematic beasts confront one another in a series of small cartouches.

The Tapestry Room ceiling is a remarkable survival, as the room has been altered a number of times over the ensuing 400 years. Its name derives from the set of Mortlake tapestries acquired by Thomas, which hung densely here until 1919. Now the room contains just one, but what a splendid example it is, made by François van Maelsack in Brussels. This piece was acquired by Edmund and Marion, and was an inspired choice. Not only is it a perfect fit for the room and in wonderful condition, but was woven at the same time as the ceiling was decorated. In the centre of the biblical scene stands Joseph, who had been sold into slavery by his brothers and who now confronts them. They huddle together looking surprised, horrified and confused. Around is a luxuriant border of fruit and flowers interspersed with cartouches containing subjects taken from Aesop's fables, cleverly linking the tapestry design to that of the ceiling.

Another of the first-floor rooms has not so much been altered as transported. Thomas's building work would have demolished a room lined with unusually crisp linen-fold panelling dating from his great-grandfather's time. Destroying this would have run counter to his antiquarian leanings, so he took the panelling down, creating a new space for it in the far south-east corner. In the centre of this room now stands a tester bed, one of the most ornamental forms of late-sixteenth-century furniture. This example is inlaid and carved with bosses, has inset panels and beautifully turned posts. It looks very snug, with its low 'roof', thick high mattress and the added privacy of drawn curtains at night.

Opposite: The Tapestry Room created in the early 17th century by Sir Thomas Brudenell, later 1st Earl of Cardigan. The tapestry by van Maelsack hangs on the far wall.

Thomas's marriage to Mary Tresham brought two collections to Deene. The first (and I admit this is somewhat speculative) is the charming set of twelve portraits that now line the lower walls of the Drawing Room. These are by an anonymous artist working around 1600. His tight linear style and love of flat colouring suggest that he also practised as a miniaturist. Whilst there is no proof that these pictures depict members of the Tresham family, it has long been thought to be the case. The second collection requires no documentary proof, being the Tresham Library; the books themselves are stamped with their arms. The library came to Deene after the death of Thomas Tresham, and stayed here until the Civil War when it was confiscated by Parliamentary soldiers in 1642. Many books have since returned and in recent years Edmund has made it his task to reacquire volumes that continue to be refugees elsewhere. The subject matter of the books ranges widely, with a good corpus of late-sixteenth-century Italian and French books on classical architecture. This provided the source material for Tresham's own buildings. More recently the inspiration for an obelisk to herald

Above: *The Drawing
Room dating from
the early 19th century
hung with portraits
of the Brudenell and
Tresham families.*

Opposite: *The Library
in the Bow Room.*

the new millennium, built by Edmund and Marion at the top of rising land to
the north of the house, was derived from another treatise in the library.

Thomas died in 1663, aged 75, his wife passing away the following year. A last
glimpse is caught of them attending the ceremonies that surrounded Charles
II's coronation. During the Civil War Thomas was often imprisoned, or else
in hiding in Wales, his estates sequestrated and his finances ruined. During
the Protectorate he had lived quietly at Deene, but at the Restoration he was
summoned to London. Charles II honoured his father's promise to grant Lord
Brudenell an earldom, and on the day before his crowning in Westminster Abbey
the king came in great state from the Tower of London to the Banqueting Hall at
Whitehall, where the diarist John Evelyn witnessed him creating six new earls
and six new barons:

> The Earl of Bedford carried the cap and the coronet, the Earl of Warwick
> the sword, the Earl of Newport the mantle. The Heralds in the gorgeous
> raiment went before, and the Garter King of Arms presented the Patents
> to the Lord Chamberlain. The King, after they had been read by the

Secretary of State, delivered each in turn to the Lords created who were
then robed, the King himself putting on their coronets and collars. After
the ceremony they were placed on each side of the thrown, the barons
holding their coronets in the hands, the Earls keeping theirs on their
heads as cousins to the King.

The following day, the new Earl and Countess of Cardigan attended the coronation service and the great banquet that followed in Westminster Hall before
returning to Deene in their coach.

Given the 1st Earl of Cardigan's longevity it is not surprising to discover that his eldest son and heir, Robert, was nearly 60 when he inherited. He enjoyed an even longer life than his father, dying in 1703 at the age of 92. His protracted reign was remarkably uneventful, and it was not until the succession of his young grandson, George, as 3rd Lord Cardigan that the pace began to change. His full-length portrait could not be less like that of the 1st Earl. Here is a young man, resplendent in peer's robes, his left hand resting on his coronet and with the outline of Westminster Abbey (before the addition of Hawksmoor's towers) in the background. The young Lord Cardigan had been in Rome when he heard of his grandfather's death some six weeks previously. He decided not to rush his return. Indeed, he stayed away for three more years before arriving back with a 'very old and ugly' Venetian mistress in tow. In the summer of 1706 he drove down to Deene and arranged an enormous house party for his friends. Whilst money was clearly no object, judging by the long list of food and wine that appears in the account books, it was unusual for such a large estate to have to buy fruit – 'apricots, pears and plums' from the gardens at nearby Blatherwick and 'apricots, grapes and figs' from Bulwick. Cardigan decided to rectify this and he employed Mr van der Meulen to survey the old gardens at Deene and advise on new. The result is the fine walled gardens, lined with brick to intensify the summer heat and thus ripen the fruit. They soon had the desired effect, and nine years later the steward, one Dan Easton, reports 'a very great quantity of both fruit of all sorts and kitchen stuffs in the gardens' and that Lord Cardigan had the finest melons in the district (whereas Lord Exeter's gardener at Burghley had 'lost almost all his melons and other fruit').

Cardigan lived a far more cosmopolitan life than his ancestors. He renounced his inherited Catholic faith and took up offices, including Master of the Buckhounds to Queen Anne. During the London season, he lived at Cardigan House in Lincoln's Inn Fields. The principal changes he made at Deene were to the landscape surrounding the house. A canal was dug out to the south-west, which may explain why the gardens veer off in that direction today. This was crossed by a stone bridge, and beyond a lake, fed by the Wilham Brook, was created, complete with a smart green sailing boat delivered from nearby Oundle. Trees were planted, either in ordered clumps or in avenues, and walks and drives constructed. Deene was literally surrounded by pleasure grounds, where the family might disport themselves on long summer days. In the autumn, their time was spent in the saddle chasing the fox, or playing bowls on a newly laid-out green, and if it was wet there was always the latest arrival – a full-sized billiard table, set up in what is now the Chapel.

It is remarkable how the gardens at Deene have been revived in the last thirty years. To the east, rich grasslands interposed with wild flowers and shaded by mighty trees lead across the park to the church. To the south, along the front of the house, is a newly devised parterre, its geometric design taken from the strapwork decoration found inside the house, and richly planted with roses, late-flowering lavender and idiosyncratically clipped topiary. The parterre leads to a terrace from which steps run down to the Wilham Brook, now widened to the scale of a small river. Beyond there are herbaceous borders, leading to a succession of gardens and van der Meulen's brick-lined garden that still provides produce for the house. Walking through these varied spaces, you derive at least as much pleasure as Lord and Lady Cardigan did in the 1720s.

When Lord Cardigan died in 1732, the estate passed to his eldest son, George. During his long tenure the focus of family life shifted to London and Deene became more a place for intermittent peaceful retirement. Initially, the new 4th Earl sought to make his mark at Deene, modernizing the east side of the south front shortly after taking over. He lowered the late-sixteenth-century turrets, removing their cupolas in the process and taking out the old-fashioned casements, which he replaced with modish sash windows. But it was perhaps the prospect of his wife's inheritance that thereafter absorbed his attention.

His was a spectacularly good match even by the standards of the day. In 1730 he had married Lady Mary Montagu, the daughter and ultimate heir of his neighbour, the Duke of Montagu. Over the next thirty years both the Duke's neighbouring estate at Boughton and Montagu House (overlooking the Thames at Westminster) became theirs. George Brudenell, 4th Earl of Cardigan, even gave up his surname to inherit, becoming not only a Montagu but also Duke of

Opposite: The recently created parterre garden, its design based on strapwork decoration found in the house.

Opposite: *Lady Mary Montagu, Countess of Cardigan, and later Duchess of Montagu (1711-1775) by Sir Joshua Reynolds P.R.A.*

Montagu, as George III re-created the title for him. Today his likeness can be found at Deene in a portrait by Herman van der Myn hanging in the Library, as can the forthright image of his wife, hanging in pride of place above the fireplace. This is a well-observed and spirited performance by Sir Joshua Reynolds. The artist opts for a seated pose, familiar from dozens of portraits by his contemporaries, but he gives it a sense of immediacy as Lady Cardigan sits erect, leaving clear space between her and the back of her chair. She looks intently at the viewer, the beautifully rendered folds in her elegant clothes taking a secondary place to her strongly characterized personality. Cleverly, Reynolds puts a small area on the left of her face into shadow, giving the impression she has just turned to observe (but probably not to speak to) you.

The new Duke and Duchess were fortunate in many things, although not with their children. Two daughters died in infancy whilst their son and heir, the handsome Lord Montheimer, died suddenly when only 25. This left a single daughter, Lady Elizabeth, who married Henry, Duke of Buccleugh and Queensberry, and thus Boughton passed out of the Brudenell family. Deene, however, was inherited first by the duke's brother, James Brudenell, and then, in 1811, by his nephew Robert, 5th Earl of Cardigan. The return of the family brought in its wake a flurry of building activity that had been in abeyance for nearly a hundred years.

In 1800 the house was still a cluster of buildings around a Great Hall; a run of small rooms, some up staircases and others along passages, decorated with plasterwork ceilings and lit through panes of stained glass. This, though, was neither the Gothick fantasy of Horace Walpole, nor the antiquarian dreamings of Sir Walter Scott, but the historic house of a distinguished family that could trace its roots with ease into the Middle Ages. So when it was at last decided to enlarge the house, to bring it up to date, great care was taken to protect these ancient qualities. The impressive new wing that was added along the south front provided three large rooms; the principal Dining Room, a Drawing Room and a bowed Library. Whilst these were fitted out in a restrained classical style, without allusion to the early architecture of the house, their exterior was sensitively contrived in the Tudor style. Here turrets and crenelated battlements enliven the well-proportioned façade and create a harmonious front to the earlier buildings behind.

The rooms have this same sense of propriety, particularly the Dining Room, with its deep frieze of alternating antheniums and wreaths. Below hang a series of large pictures by the best early-nineteenth-century equestrian artist, John Ferneley, depicting Lord Cardigan's hunters, brood mares and foals. Ferneley was a local artist, discovered by the Duke of Rutland; he later trained under Ben Marshall before trying his luck in Ireland. There he developed his style and when he returned to England he established his studio in Melton Mowbray, at the heart of the hunting country. One of his great canvases at Deene shows the hunters in the park, the house with its new wing complete in the background. Its pair shows a

Mary D.^r & Co-heiress
John Duke of Montague
Wife of Geo. E.^l Cardigan
Ob. 1775

similar scene at Melton Mowbray, where the 5th Lord Cardigan kept a hunting box. This is one of the finest groups of Ferneley's works in England, hung as intended, amongst rich mahogany furniture and with a dining table laden with silver, thick-cut Regency glass and, in this case, a Spode service painted tangerine and cobalt blue. From the Dining Room, you can step into the Staircase Hall, which links this part of the house to the Great Hall beyond and provides access to the new bedrooms above. It dates from the same time as the new wing and was cleverly created out of the former open courtyard. Although painted cream, it is known as the White Hall – it is one of the trials of English country houses that rooms seldom match the colours they are named after! Today it is devoted to the life and career of James Thomas Brudenell, 7th Earl of Cardigan (1797–1868), the most famous (or perhaps infamous) holder of the title.

The large paintings hanging on opposite walls seem to reflect Lord Cardigan's opposing reputations. On the left, halfway up the stairs, is George Henry Laporte's depiction of *The Battle of Balaclava, 25th October 1854*. In the centre of the scene, Lord Cardigan (in a uniform he designed himself) gallops forward astride his charger, Ronald, brandishing his sword. He has just led his troops, the Light

Brigade, down the treacherous valley with the Russian guns firing down from either side. He had followed orders delivered in the heat of battle by a young officer, Captain Nolan, who could not be quizzed as to the instruction as he was killed be an enemy shell straight after relaying it. Without hesitation Lord Cardigan sprang into his action, leading his men through the enemy bombardment as if following hounds with the Quorn.

Arriving at the far end of the valley after a charge of some ten minutes, he was assailed by yet more Russian artillery and nearly toppled from Ronald by two Cossacks. He just managed to stay mounted, turned and rode back whence he came with his remaining men. As a military manoeuvre the charge gained nothing, but as an example of sheer courage, it galvanized the whole British Army, and eleven days later they fought and won the decisive battle of the Crimean War, the battle of Inkerman. Shortly afterwards Cardigan returned home, passing through the Black Sea and the Mediterranean aboard his private yacht *The Caradoc*. He was understandably uncertain as to the reception waiting for him – would he be hailed as a hero, or as a martinet who had followed his own judgement and to hell with the consequences? He had, since the 1820s, acquired a reputation for the latter and the scales were finely balanced. He continued homeward at a leisurely pace until he reached Marseilles, where he heard that the Houses of Parliament had passed a resolution 'expressing their thanks for your distinguished conduct in the brilliant operations in which you have taken part in the Crimea'. The public mood had been captured by the poet laureate, Lord Tennyson, whose famous poem begins:

> *Half a league, half a league*
> *Half a league onward*
> *All in the Valley of Death*
> *Rode the six hundred*
> *Forward the Light Brigade!*
> *'Charge for the guns!' he said*
> *Into the Valley of Death*
> *Rode the six hundred*

And ended in the sixth verse with:

> *When can their glory fade?*
> *O the wild charge they made!*
> *All the world wondered*
> *Honour the charge they made!*
> *Honour the Light Brigade!*
> *Noble Six Hundred.*

When he returned to Deene, Cardigan was fêted by the whole county. He arrived in Northampton by train and from the station his carriage was pulled through

the streets to strains of 'Hail the Conquering Hero Comes'. He was presented with an address of welcome 124ft 4in in length, with somewhere between 4,000 and 5,000 signatures on it. This is preserved in one of the cabinets in the White Hall together with a host of other memorabilia, including his specially designed uniforms. One of the most touching objects is a photograph of Ronald at Lord Cardigan's funeral in 1868. Standing stock still, with his master's boots turned to face the rear, the elderly horse had fallen asleep, woken by an enterprising soldier sounding the charge. He was then led by two grooms, following immediately behind the coffin. The *Northampton Mercury* described the scene: 'The presence of the noble animal was a most touching constituent of the mournful procession. It moved with a solemn and dignified step, as if with a consciousness of the occasion'. After Ronald died a few years later, his head was preserved and it is displayed here, together with a hoof (two others remain, one in the Royal Collection, the other in the Regimental Museum, but the fourth has since vanished).

Opposite: *James, 7th Earl of Cardigan (1797–1868) on his charger, Ronald, leading the Charge of the Light Brigade in 1854 by Alfred de Prades.*

Above: *Lord Cardigan describing the Charge of the Light Brigade to the Prince Consort and the Royal Children by James Sant, 1855.*

Hanging on the far wall of the White Hall is James Sant's *Lord Cardigan Explaining the Battle to the Prince Consort and the Royal Children*. It was only three days after his return that the Earl was summoned to Windsor Castle by Queen Victoria. On the third day of his visit, the queen recalled in her diary, 'After breakfast we took the children into the corridor to see Lord Cardigan who explained again the whole of his experiences to them'. The slightly strange thing about the painting is the absence of the queen. Perhaps she felt that, despite his heroism, it was inappropriate for her to be painted standing next to him. He was a notorious ladies' man who had abandoned his first wife and was now living openly with his mistress. And what a mistress! Adeline de Horsey, with her jet-black hair, wasp waist and flagrant disregard for convention. The portraits by Richard Buckner and Alfred de Prades make no attempt to disguise her radiant attractions. When the first Lady Cardigan died in 1858 Adeline became his second countess and it was she who was responsible for commissioning the royal sculptor, Edgar Boehn, to design the monumental, flamboyant tomb of her husband. When this was unveiled, many were shocked to see beside the body of Lord Cardigan the figure of the young new Lady Cardigan, decked out in peeress's robes, holding a cross which dangled from a double row of pearls and staring longingly at her husband. Adeline long outlived him and stories abound of her later activities: bicycling around the estate in his famous cherry-picker trousers; dying her hair blonde; trying out her own coffin in the hall; proposing marriage to Benjamin Disraeli; and keeping her Brudenell in-laws at bay. All of them are true.

After her death in 1915 the estates passed to the grandson of the 9th Earl of Cardigan, Ernest, and then to his brother, George Brudenell. It is George's son and his wife, Edmund and Marion Brudenell, who have lived at Deene for the past fifty years. At the beginning of their time, the famous Northamptonshire historian Joan Wake published *The Brudenells of Deene*. As an account of the family it will never be bettered, but its illustrations are hard to credit. They show Deene a casualty of wartime damage. 'By 1945 the already dilapidated house was virtually derelict, exceedingly uncomfortable and the roof leaked. There was dry rot, little plumbing and neither heating nor electricity and the kitchen was so distant that Mrs Brudenell used to ride there on a bicycle'. The Great Hall, almost bereft of furniture, was a gaunt, chilly space; the landings and even the Library were sparsely furnished and the carpets threadbare. Edmund and Marion's achievements are all the more remarkable when seen against this background. They have bought back the warmth and character of the house, and they have made it into an oasis of fun for family and friends. What is more, they have brought Adeline de Horsey in from the cold. After her death, her memory was expunged; old photographs of her were put away and her florid brass bed was sold. This resurfaced recently in a local sale and Edmund and Marion bought it, restoring it to her old bedroom. The rich mixture of history that forms Deene can certainly accommodate such a game bird!

Goodwood, Sussex

The seat of the Duke of Richmond and Lennox

Previous page:
Goodwood from the Park.

It is from high up on the South Downs, midway between Midhurst and Chichester, that what first attracted the 1st Duke of Richmond to this part of England becomes stunningly apparent. The landscape is breathtaking. Steep hills drop away on all sides, grassland descends into deep valleys before rising through woods to equally high ground. It was fast hunting country: horses and riders hurtling pell-mell in pursuit of fox and deer. The small village of Charlton, tucked away in the valley below, was the Melton Mowbray of the late seventeenth century, a favourite haunt of a bevy of dukes and half the Knights of the Garter. They were joined in the early 1690s by the young illegitimate son of Charles II, Charles Lennox, 1st Duke of Richmond (1672–1723). As he had no property in the district he took a house owned by the local magnate, the Duke of Northumberland, that had been built in the early seventeenth century. A few years later, he bought that house: Goodwood. Although not his intention, it would develop over the next century from a plain and old-fashioned hunting box into a grand country house that has prospered in the hands of his successors ever since. The same energy and enterprise that took the young duke whistling across the Downs still runs in the veins of his descendants. Goodwood is one of the most active and forward-looking estates in the country.

Although only 25 when he acquired the property, Charles Lennox had already been a duke for twenty-two years. He enjoyed an enviable financial position with an annual stipend of £2,000 and revenues derived from coal exported from Newcastle upon Tyne. Although not the eldest of the king's illegitimate sons, he was the one most favoured by his father, whose royal generosity was stimulated by his clever and ambitious mother, Louise de Keroualle, Duchess of Portsmouth. Louise, a dark-haired beauty of 21, had caught the eye of the 50-year-old king in 1670 when she accompanied his sister Henrietta, Duchess

Charles Lennox, 1st Duke of Richmond (1672–1723) when a boy, wearing the Robes of the Order of the Garter by Willem Wissing.

of Orléans, from Paris to Dover. Their royal rendezvous acted as camouflage to a secret treaty signed between Charles II and his Catholic cousin, Louis XIV. Louise went back to France but, following the duchess's death three weeks later, returned to England – Louis XIV wanted a reliable spy at the English court and Charles II was looking for consolation following the loss of his sister. Louise and the king became better acquainted at a race meeting at Newmarket, and Charles Lennox was the outcome.

In the Ballroom at Goodwood hangs a fine group of portraits of the young duke's relations, arranged around a huge painting of his grandparents, Charles I and Queen Henrietta Maria. In the foreground stands the young Prince Charles and the Princess Mary, his elder sister, sits on her mother's lap. This was Van Dyck's first work for the king, painted during the summer of 1632, and the prime version is still in the Royal Collection. That at Goodwood was painted shortly afterwards and is thought to have originally hung in the Queen's Apartments

at Somerset House. Opposite, between the windows, hangs the mature image of Charles II and tucked away in the corner is the ravishing painting of his youngest sister the Princess Henrietta, Duchess of Orléans. This was painted by Sir Peter Lely and shows the artist at his most dazzling. The princess turns towards the viewer, calm and serene, a counterfoil to her shimmering dress, its radiant colours caught in raking light. Her modesty is a contrast to the lasciviousness of Louise de Keroualle, caught in a portrait by the French artist Henri Gascars, who followed her to England. Here she is pretending to be Venus, the Goddess of Love, her long dark hair falling loose about her shoulders as she lolls on a day bed and fondles a dove whilst a young cupid appears to be pushing her into action.

The result of Louise's amorous royal encounters, the young Duke of Richmond, was painted twice by Willem Wissing. That at the end of the room

Above: *The Ballroom, originally designed by James Wyatt circa 1800 and completed by Elliott's of Chichester.*

Opposite: *Charles I, Queen Henrietta Maria and their eldest children Charles, Prince of Wales and Mary, Princess Royal. A composition by Sir Anthony Van Dyck.*

is clearly more concerned with his status than his character. He sits astride a stool wearing the full panoply of a Knight of the Garter, his left leg bent forward to show off the Garter itself whilst his large ceremonial hat sits to the left, resplendent with its bending plumes. His was a position worth celebrating. He was made a Knight of the Garter at the age of nine, and Charles II had earlier bestowed on him those titles that belonged to his only paternal cousin, Charles Stuart, Duke of Richmond and Lennox, who died in the year of his birth. Richmond was an ancient English royal title, enjoyed, for instance, by John of Gaunt, whereas Lennox was the title of his Stuart forebears. According to the diarist John Evelyn, the new duke was 'a very pretty boy' and he grew up to do little but enjoy his semi-royal status. After Charles II's death he and Louise vacillated between France and England but, unlike his mother, he settled permanently in London in 1692. That year he also married Anne Brudenell, the sister of George, 3rd Earl of Cardigan, of Deene Park and in due course had three children (one of whom, Louisa, married James, 3rd Earl of Berkeley). Richmond held a series of court appointments under William III, Queen Anne and George I, although these were largely sinecures, but he lived in great style at Richmond House in Whitehall, escaping down to Goodwood to hunt whenever possible. It was here, much ruined by drink, that he died in 1723. As a royal duke with no landed seat, his body was taken back to London to be buried

in Henry VII's chapel at Westminster Abbey. It is telling that just a quarter of a century later he would be reinterred in Chichester cathedral: Goodwood had become by then that landed seat.

His heir, Charles Lennox, 2nd Duke of Richmond (1701–1750), was responsible for this change. In common with all the eldest sons of the family, he was named after his royal ancestor. He was a much steadier character than his father and it is not surprising that when only eighteen he did not take kindly to a paternal instruction to marry a 13-year-old, Lady Sarah Cadogan, in order to discharge his father's gambling debts to the girl's father. Nevertheless, this is exactly what happened at Lord Cadogan's residence in The Hague on 4 December 1719. Immediately afterwards the groom left, on his own, for an extended Grand Tour, visiting France, Austria and Italy, and did not return to England for three years. During that time he became something of a connoisseur of the arts, collecting paintings and sculpture and developing a passion for Italian opera. Soon after his return he attended a performance and was struck by an enchanting girl, surrounded by admirers, in an adjacent box. Enquiring of his friends who she was, he was surprised to learn it was his wife, 'the toast of London'. And, despite its inauspicious start, the marriage proved particularly happy.

As a young man the 2nd Duke was a keen cricketer, a game then in its fledgling state. He arranged matches in the mid 1720s with his neighbour, Sir William Gage, and in 1727 with Mr Broderick of Peper Harrow in Sussex. He drew up the first formal rules of the game for this match, and the document is still at Goodwood. It is brilliantly concise. Having dealt with runs, overs and wickets in just a few short paragraphs, he then included the most important statement – if there is any disagreement it can be settled only 'by the Duke or Mr Broderick'. This no-nonsense approach amuses the current duke. It presumably still comes in extremely handy when he

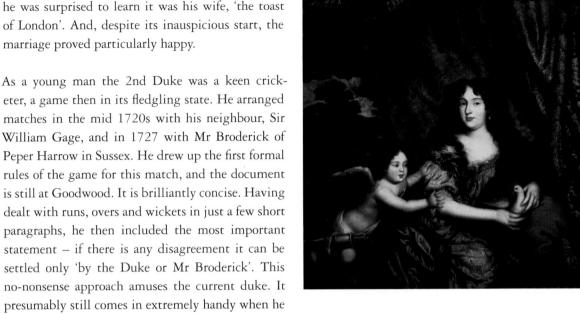

arranges matches at Goodwood to commemorate his ancestor's pivotal role in establishing the game. Such matches are played using only two stumps and a single bail, in the fashion of the eighteenth century. It is therefore possible for a ball to pass clean between the stumps. Should this happen, the batsman is deemed not out. You can imagine the look of pained irritation on the bowler's face! The cricket ground lies to the south-east of the house, now with a charming thatched pavilion and bordered by fields where a variety of cattle graze (part of the estate's large organically reared herd).

Cricket was an occasional fair-weather sport, but hunting was a regular activity during the winter months. The duke had taken over the management of the Charlton Hunt in the 1720s and at the end of the decade commissioned Roger Morris to build him a house in the village so that he could avoid the long hack home over the Downs. This house, delightfully named Fox Hall, survives (now owned by the Landmark Trust). It is a handsome block, built of brick and dressed stone in the Palladian style that would have appealed to another of Morris's other main patrons, the Earl of Burlington. The interior is designed to fulfil the duke's needs: a ground floor with a series of small rooms where his supper might be prepared and his clothes freshened, and above,

extending through two storeys, a single large chamber – the bedroom where
he could sleep off the excesses of the day. Behind the house is a courtyard and
a gaunt brick stable block, redolent of tacking up and rubbing down. There is
something beguiling about this man who knew what he wanted and arranged
matters accordingly. Although not everything went to plan. When he constructed his menagerie in the park, now gone except for some underground passages
and a monument to a favourite lioness, his steward reported that 'we are very
much troubled with Rude Company to see ye animals. Sunday last we had 4 or 5
hundred good and bad'. A large crowd, but where else in the locality could you
see wolves, tigers, lions, leopards, an armadillo and a 'woman tygerr'?

The 2nd Duke also made alterations to Goodwood itself. An initial ambitious
rebuilding project was abandoned in favour of remodelling. Roger Morris re-
designed the centre of the old house, creating the Long Hall from a series of
rooms. You now approach its fine entrance across an internal courtyard, caught
in a medley of later architecture. Standing among irregularly placed sash windows and a rich pattern of local flints, its design strikes you as ordered and
self-confident. Two tall semi columns ending in crisply carved Corinthian capitals support a high entablature with the duke's Garter nonchalantly pinned to
the wall above. Inside, the 2nd Duke's Hall has survived later alterations. Out
of an unpromising space Morris created a beautifully balanced room. It is articulated by two pairs of matching mahogany doors, a duo of matching marble
fireplaces, a quartet of niches for the antiquities collected in Rome and two Ionic

screens that cross the end of the room, disguising the irregularity of the space. It is English Palladianism at its best: bold and unfussy. Recently the room has been hung with some of the Italian paintings the 2nd Duke acquired on his Grand Tour, together with his most significant later purchase, the London views by Canaletto.

Canaletto was already well known to the duke before his arrival in London in May 1746. Richmond had acquired ten of the tomb paintings of Whig heroes, to which the artist had contributed, as well as two sparkling views of the Grand Canal in Venice. These commissions had been arranged in the 1720s through a likeable Irish rogue, Owen McSwiney. McSwiney was also in London in the summer of 1746, where he bumped into the duke's former tutor, Thomas Hill. Hill reported to the duke that the Irishman, whom he described as 'almost drunk', had received a letter from Canaletto asking for an introduction. The timing was opportune. Richmond House, which had been purchased (and named) by the 1st Duke, had just been rebuilt and the second duke was also in high spirits, having returned the previous year from Scotland a military hero after playing a major role in crushing the Jacobite rebellion. The resulting meeting led to a commission of two pictures celebrating the views from the first floor of Richmond House: *Whitehall and the Privy Garden from the Drawing Room* and *The Thames and the City of London from the Dining Room*. These are large canvasses and demonstrate not only the artist's brilliance as a topographer but also his keen observation of the English in their native setting.

In the right foreground of the first painting is the new Palladian stable block of Richmond House in the lower right corner, with a liveried servant bowing to a higher official and other servants entering a doorway where chickens are scratching for grubs. To the left is the Old Privy Garden of Whitehall Palace (the old royal palace destroyed by fire in January 1698). These gardens were reserved for the use of neighbours and their friends, and here the artist depicts the gentlemen standing round chatting whilst the ladies sally forth in their wide panniered skirts. He is almost showing off: a smudge of blue here, a shade of pink there and just a little white captures not just the look but also the character of a passing lady of fashion. Beyond the garden wall is Whitehall itself, the thoroughfare that linked the mercantile life of the City to the political activity of Westminster. In its centre stands the ancient Tudor gateway known as the Holbein Gate, which was pulled down shortly afterwards, and Inigo Jones's great Banqueting House, which still dominates the scene today. Just behind it the spire of the newly built St Martin in the Fields and the cupola of Northumberland House are visible.

Canaletto's genius lies in his ability to capture a scene in such a way that no element in it feels forced or artificial. There is no incident here that could jar the relaxed spaciousness of the composition, and the same is true of his *View of the Thames*. What a view! Over half the canvas is taken up by the river and the sky providing a subtle foil to the remainder of the scene. The Thames is enlivened

by small craft bobbing about in the rippling water, and the sky by slowly rising clouds taking the smoke of London heavenward. Holding the composition together are variegated blocks of colour; the green of the grass and trees on the far bank and in the garden below the Inns of Court; the pink of the pantiles and bricks; and the off-white of Portland stone. Dominating the skyline is St Paul's Cathedral, surrounded by the city churches of Wren and his followers. Two guild barges, decked out with gilded woodwork and painted roofs, are being ferried along the river by pairs of oarsmen in the cleanest white shirts. Small rowing boats run passengers back and forth – there being only one permanent crossing of the river at that time: London Bridge. Canaletto shows characteristic restraint in both these views. You might have expected a procession of the ducal family on the terrace, yet he just provides a steady flow of people with a solitary sweeper at work at Montagu House next door. These are two supreme mid-eighteenth-century views of the city: no other artist achieved Canaletto's brilliance.

As he turned back into the rooms at Richmond House, Canaletto would have surveyed an equally beguiling scene with Old Master paintings in gilt frames hung against dark-coloured fabrics, pedestals topped with antique sculpture and richly carved gilded furniture. Some of these pieces are now at Goodwood, including the marble fireplaces in the Music Room and the Reception Room, and a pair of richly carved chairs which were bought back by Lord March, the present duke's son, in 1996. The design of these, like the fireplaces, is attributed to William Kent, who began to invent wholly novel furniture in the 1720s, probably working first for Sir Robert Walpole at Houghton. His furniture reflects his years of study in Italy; a highly wrought synthesis between the late baroque style of Andrea Brustolon and Giovanni Giardini and his own whimsical use of classical ornament. The armchairs have gilded arms that ripple with carved scales, and the legs are formed from broken scrolls linked to an apron with a bizarre pendant cartouche. On both sides of their upholstered backs are carved heads and the centres are taken by one of his favourite motifs, a large scallop shell. Great care was taken to keep the swell of the upholstery to a minimum, and the small nail heads act as a neat frame to differentiate one part from another. The chairs are every bit as exuberant as the Walpole furniture at Houghton, providing a telling reminder of the equally rich taste of the 2nd Duke at Richmond House.

Opposite: *London and the River Thames from Richmond House in Westminster by Canaletto.*

Above: *A pair of giltwood chairs commissioned by the 2nd Duke of Richmond for Richmond House in London, the design attributed to William Kent.*

The 2nd Duke died unexpectedly of an inflammation of the bladder whilst passing through Godalming on his way to Goodwood in the summer of 1750. He was only 41. His inconsolable wife followed him to an early grave the next year. Two of their daughters were by then married. Lady Caroline had eloped with Henry Fox in 1744 and four years had passed before a family reconciliation, aided by her gift to her parents of a specially commissioned Meissen box that opened to reveal her portrait. In 1747 Lady Emilia married the less rumbustious Duke of Leinster. The 2nd Duke's heir was another Charles, then aged 15. He inherited not only Goodwood but also his father's last building project: an incomplete large new wing designed by Matthew Brettingham attached to the south of the original house.

During his minority the 3rd Duke took the Grand Tour, visiting Germany, Switzerland, France and Italy and developing his innate interest in the arts and architecture which was to blossom into a lifetime of patronage. His first architectural undertaking mirrored that of his father, although on a grander scale. He commissioned Sir William Chambers to complete Brettingham's house and to build a vast stable block to the south of the house, able to accommodate fifty-four

horses. This building almost dwarfed Brettingham's block; its vast courtyard was entered through an impressive triumphal arch and each of its flanks was further articulated with pedimented entrances. Its building underlined the fact that sport was still the principal activity at Goodwood, emphasized in the duke's next important commission: three paintings by George Stubbs in 1759–60.

Stubbs' works now hang in the Entrance Hall. They depict the family enjoying hunting, shooting and racing. In the first, the duke, who had reinstated the Charlton pack in 1757, is shown in the centre with his brother, Lord George. Both are mounted. Liveried hunt servants with his pack of hounds are in the foreground, whilst in the distance, under an ethereal group of trees, huntsmen and hounds start to gallop down the hillside in the direction of the Sussex coast beyond. The artist had recently completed his exhaustive studies of the anatomy of the horse, giving him the ability to paint the animals in an infinitely more realistic way than his English predecessors. This newly acquired skill is also to be seen in the other two works. The second picture shows the duke's rather stout brother-in-law, Henry Holland, out shooting with the duke's cousin, George Keppel, Earl of Albemarle. They are shown, guns in hand, walking up towards the wood, whilst liveried servants attend with their second guns and beautifully observed horses. The gun dogs are beginning to become impatient, as if sensing what is about to happen; adding a liveliness to the scene. In the final canvas the ladies of the house make their appearance. In the centre the new duchess, Lady Mary Bruce, is talking to the steward whilst her sister-in-law, Lady George Lennox, is shown in profile to the right. Again Stubbs animates the painting through the activity of their animals: one of the horses turns its neck whilst the other stretches down to lick its outstretched leg. On either side race horses are in

training: three to the left wearing liveried blankets are being exercised and on the right a fine grey is being rubbed down with straw after having been put through its paces. The painting is full of lively incident, from the small dog unable to resist the pleasure of matching the speed of the horses to the wonderfully observed small boy clutching a huge pile of straw. These are pictures born of an easy familiarity with life at Goodwood and it comes as no surprise to find that Stubbs was a guest there between 1759 and 1760. He painted for the young duke the finest works of his early maturity.

During the 1750s the 3rd Duke was often with the British army on the continent, seeing action at the battle of Minden in 1759 (the same year that his portrait was painted by Sir Joshua Reynolds). In 1760 he gave up active service and entered politics, leading in due course to his appointment as ambassador in Paris. This provided him with an unexpected opportunity to see for himself the latest French works of art, a privilege that had been denied to British travellers during the Seven Years War. As with his patronage of Chambers and Stubbs, in France Richmond was his own man. From the Sèvres manufacturers he commissioned a unique dining service with not one but two ground colours, blue and green. And that was not all. He requested that the ornithological decoration should accurately depict real birds, rather than the imaginative confections usually found on Sèvres porcelain. He took George Edwards' *A Natural History of Uncommon Birds* (a book dedicated to his father) to Paris and requested that the porcelain decorators Aloncle and Chappuis copy its colour illustrations – although he would not leave the book with them; they had to bring the delicate porcelain to the embassy. This service is now displayed in the cabinets in the Card Room, looking as pristine as when ordered, probably on his visit to the factory on 12 November 1765. Through this singular act, the Duke became the most significant English patron of the Sèvres factory.

Whilst in Paris the duke also bought furniture by the city's leading manufacturers: including chairs by Delanois and a dressing table by Roger Vandercruse. But he was given the four large Gobelin tapestries by the French king depicting episodes from the life of Cervantes' hero Don Quixote. Designed by Antoine Coypel and made by the weavers Audran and Cozette, they formed part of the series of hangings ordered by Louis XV for his château at Marly. The tapestries are startlingly novel. Each episode from the Don's life is treated as a picture, surrounded by elaborate borders incorporating flowers and birds set against a pale buff colour to imitate a wall and with further borders beyond. In this way they respond to and extend the architectural decoration of a room, rather than replacing it in the manner of their baroque predecessors.

During the 1760s the duke was also active in buying land at Goodwood including the Halnaker and Westhampnett estates. The park was expanded to 1,000 acres and planted with exotic trees, including cedars of Lebanon. He also turned his attention to the house and commissioned James Wyatt to plan a large new block. The initial plan fizzled out in the mid 1770s, a victim of Wyatt's architectural ambition and the duke's shortage of money, although not before a new Drawing Room had been built running off the Long Hall. It now seems rather remote from the rest of the building, the remainder of the original Jacobean house and the rest of Wyatt's early building having been demolished in the last century. Yet the journey to it is worthwhile. Here is one of the most glorious early neoclassical interiors in England. Here Wyatt incorporated the duke's French purchases. The tapestries were provided with matching slim gilt frames, with similar treatment given to the gilded dado and skirting. The ceiling was decorated with a delicate geometric pattern of classical ornament executed by Joseph Rose, picked out in greens, blue, pinks and pale yellows (now matched by a recently woven carpet). In the centre the duke commissioned a delicate and cleverly contrived chimney piece designed and made by John Bacon. A young

Opposite: *The Tapestry Drawing Room designed by James Wyatt in the 1770s and showing the highly original marble fireplace by John Bacon A.R.A.*

Above: *A Gobelins tapestry depicting an episode from the life of Don Quixote with the Don intrigued by a talking table! Part of a set commissioned by Louis XV and given to the 3rd Duke of Richmond when Ambassador to Paris in 1765.*

man and a girl, both half naked, stand on either side eternally looking at one another. They hold aloft draperies revealing the fireplace below. Beyond the illusion is extended with the ends of the fabric held in place by rings in the wall. The whole is carved out of white marble, the two figures as separate pieces and the drapery in three sections, the joins carefully disguised by deep undercutting. Bacon's early experience as a designer of porcelain figures is apparent in the delicacy of this work. It is yet another example of the 3rd Duke's ability to identify young talent, for in the early 1770s Bacon was only just beginning to establish himself as an independent sculptor.

Opposite: The Egyptian Dining Room designed by James Wyatt circa 1805 with scagliola work by Joseph Allcott and the chairs with their crocodile backs.

It was another twenty years until Goodwood was finally transformed into the house you see today. In the end it wasn't the outcome of carefully laid plans but a response to disaster. Richmond House in Whitehall was destroyed by fire in 1791. It was on an uninsured leasehold and that fact, coupled with the duke's declining income, persuaded him not to rebuild in London but to extend his house in the country to make room for the works of art that had survived the conflagration. He abandoned ideas of further reconstruction, or even adding flanking wings to the building. Rather typically, even in his straitened circumstances, he did something more audacious. He effectively banished the earlier house to the rear of the new building and added huge new blocks to the south, running out from Brettingham's wing. At a stroke he tripled Goodwood's size, turning it to face the sea, and provided himself with large state rooms including the Picture Gallery. Again it was Wyatt who provided the plans.

A double-height loggia leads to the Entrance Hall, with a massive screen of granite columns brought by boat from Guernsey. Off to the right is the Drawing Room, hung with the royal portraits in their splendid period frames saved from Richmond House, now augmented with portraits of the duke by Reynolds, Mengs, Romney and Batoni. At the far end, in one of Wyatt's circular towers, is the Card Room and beyond that the Picture Gallery, which also serves as a ballroom. These grand rooms are decorated in Wyatt's later classical idiom, further embellished in the 1830s in the full-blown late-Regency style.

The Dining Room was the only room to be completed during the duke's lifetime and its decoration is more idiosyncratic – just as you might expect from such a patron. Obscured throughout the twentieth century by later repainting, it has recently been triumphantly restored. Its style was the duke's response to Egyptomania, the fervour that swept through Europe following Nelson's victory at the battle of Aboukir Bay and Napoleon's Egyptian campaign. Lord March, the present duke's son, who has been responsible for this restoration, is as excited by it as his ancestor. Much of the original wall surface, covered in scagliola worked by Joseph Allcott, Wyatt's craftsman, had survived under layers of later paint and the rest of the colour scheme – dark grained wood and gilded bronzes – was revealed behind an unused door. The rest of the restoration is to some extent conjectural, although great pains have been taken to use Wyatt's original

source, Baron Denon's *Planches du Voyage dans la Basse et la Haute Egypte pendant les Campaignes de Bonaparte*. The duke's copy of the first edition published in 1802 was, of course, still in the library next door. Even the chairs echo the scheme, with long bronze crocodiles, seemingly anchored in Nile mud, decorating their backs. Here, as elsewhere in the state rooms, new curtains have been specially woven to reflect the decor devised by Wyatt and his 70-year-old patron.

The 3rd Duke died in 1806 leaving an incomplete house and debts of £180,000. It is no surprise therefore that his nephew and successor, Charles, 4th Duke of Richmond, could not afford to live at Goodwood. After serving as Lord Lieutenant of Ireland he and his wife, Lady Charlotte, daughter of the Duke of Gordon, retired with their large family to live inexpensively in Brussels. The 4th Duke's portrait by Hoppner now hangs in the Red Hall amongst other military portraits, including one of the Duke of Wellington, and the cabinets there contain miniatures of dashing officers. They all look as if they might have enjoyed the dance depicted over the fireplace: and they did. That ball was given on 15

June 1815 by a rather flustered duchess. She, like everyone else in Brussels, had heard of Napoleon's rapid advance towards the city from Paris but she sought the advice of her friend Wellington, who phlegmatically said, 'Duchess you may give your Ball'. During the course of the dance, news arrived that the emperor's army had already reached the outskirts of the city. The officers had to leave directly for the battlefield at Quatre Bras, abandoning their poor hostess with her seven unmarried daughters. Two days later the two armies met in earnest at Waterloo. The 4th Duke, though over 50, formed part of Wellington's unofficial suite whilst his son, Lord March, saw action as aide-de-camp to the Prince of Orange. In the Red Hall there is also a touching memento of another hero of that day, Lord Uxbridge. Uxbridge was badly injured during the fighting, but when Wellington informed him bluntly, 'You have lost your leg, sir', coolly responded, 'By Gad, sir, so I have'. In the cabinet is his letter to his wife breaking the news a little more gently! Two years later their daughter, Lady Caroline Paget, married Lord March, who succeeded his father in 1819 after the 4th Duke, who had taken another government appointment as governor general of Canada, died from rabies contracted through a nip from a pet fox.

His duchess lived on to witness the revival of the family fortune. In 1836 her brother, the 5th and last Duke of Gordon, died, leaving the vast family estates to his nephew, her son. Overnight the fiscal cloud that had hung over the Richmonds was dispelled and by 1838 Mr Elliott, an architect from Chichester, was hard at work on the buildings left unfinished on the 3rd Duke's death. The family returned to Goodwood and over the course of the nineteenth century established Goodwood Races, bred horses and prize cattle, served in government nationally and locally, and were granted the additional title of Dukes of Gordon by Queen Victoria in 1876. Perhaps it comes as no surprise to find they made no significant changes to the house, given the time and expense it had taken to finally complete.

Since the 1960s the pace of change has quickened again. The current duke and his son, Lord March, have been busy developing both the sport and landscape which first attracted their ancestors down to Sussex. High above the Downs a series of impressive contemporary buildings surround the racecourse and the once-famous motor-racing circuit on a former airfield has recently been revived. Goodwood is once again a name synonymous with British motor racing. Hurtling round the track with Charles March you cannot help but be impressed, both by the speed with which he drives and by the speed of change here. The old kennels are to become a club house for all those who take part in the various activities on the estate. Members will undoubtedly be as comfortable as the former occupants – when built by Wyatt in the 1770s for the 3rd Duke, the hounds were kept warm by a special heating system.

Charles March relishes the challenges of Goodwood. Some of the changes are long term, such as his plans to manage the estate organically or the addition of a new entrance hall at the rear of the house. Others are more transient. I was amazed to see a photograph in his office showing a gigantic sculpture made of cars standing on the grass in front of the house. It was certainly gone by the time I visited, leaving just a telling dip in the grass. I learned it had been there only in June 2005 as part of another of his inaugurations: the annual Festival of Speed. I have no doubt that something even more spectacular will appear there next year and thereafter.

Holker Hall, Cumbria

The seat of the Lord Cavendish

It is strange how sometimes, travelling by train, you can 'find' yourself in the nineteenth century. Sitting in your carriage, you look out at a view surprisingly unchanged. You track across a landscape unexplored by twentieth-century roads before entering towns and cities as if through a back door. The journey from Lancaster along the branch line to Barrow-in-Furness gives just this sensation. You share almost the same views as did William Cavendish, 7th Duke of Devonshire, who owned Holker Hall in the nineteenth century. At Carnforth the railway line abandons the valley and sets out across open country, passing through Silverdale and then across the water as the River Kent opens up into Morecambe Bay. You catch a succession of views; first a low-lying range of hills (a prelude to the Lake District beyond) and then the widening bay with the finger of Humphrey Head pushing south. The train runs on to the nineteenth-century seaside town of Grange-over-Sands, replete with a floral clock and a gabled station, then inland, passing the seventeenth-century town of Flookburgh, to halt at the station of Cark in Cartmel.

Here you alight, as indeed generations of the Cavendish family have done since the railway was built, to take the short journey to Holker Hall. It stands surrounded by a series of gardens and parkland, with glimpses beyond of the sea to the south and the hills to the west that rise to form the Furness Fells. Standing here you can understand why the house has never been sold since it became the property of the Preston family in the sixteenth century. It has passed through their descendants, the Lowthers and the Cavendishes, to the present owners, Hugh and Grania, Lord and Lady Cavendish. In the introduction to their guidebook, they write 'Holker [is] more desirable, more favoured by Providence and more enhanced with natural beauty than any other place on earth'. The family's love for this house meant that when it was largely de-

stroyed in the late nineteenth century (just after the railway had made it more accessible), they set to rebuilding it. Holker Hall is a phoenix – a wonder born from its own ashes.

It was in the early hours of 9 March 1871 that fire broke out in the main block of the house. William, 7th Duke of Devonshire, and his family were in residence, and his second son, Lord Frederick Cavendish, was woken by a terrific crash in his dressing room adjacent to his bedroom. Opening the door he was smitten by the heat and the smoke. He raised the alarm and the family and staff all managed to reach safety, yet so rapid and destructive was the blaze that the entire main block was devastated, together with the contents:

Right: *The entrance porch in the Tudor style, designed by Paley and Austen, with the sculpted arms of the Duke of Devonshire and the date 1873.*

Opposite: *Heraldic stained glass found in the windows of the Main Hall, showing the Cavendish coat of arms.*

ancient family portraits, fine Old Masters, sculpture, English and continental furniture, works of art, and the whole of the library. Grim photographs survive to show how extensive the catastrophe was. It must have been almost overwhelming, especially for the duke, then in his sixties. He had known and loved the house all his life. His grandfather, Lord George Augustus Henry Cavendish, later 1st Earl of Burlington (1754–1834), had inherited Holker from a bachelor uncle in 1802, six years before William was born. The death of his father when he was only five meant that he spent part of his childhood there, and it was to Holker in 1829 that he brought his young bride, Lady Blanche Howard, daughter of the Earl of Carlisle. Five years later William inherited the estate and by 1838 he had instructed Websters of Kendal to redesign the main block the better to accommodate his growing family. Websters produced a pleasant if unadventurous Tudor-bethan block, with an enfilade of rooms along the principal façade looking over the gardens.

Sadly, it was not to be enjoyed by Lady Blanche, who died aged just 28 in 1840 before the building work was completed. Happily, her posthumous portrait painted by John Lucas survived the fire and now hangs in pride of place on the staircase. It not only provides a good likeness of this gentle and unaffected lady but also speaks of her character. This is no flashy, metropolitan portrait. Like her husband, she enjoyed the seclusion of the estate, away from the noise and bustle of London. She sits, or rather perches, on a bench, wearing a simple white dress with mauve shawl, her hair combed but not artificially dressed. Beyond, Lucas sketches an evocation of the countryside around Holker. It might have been with memories of those early happy days that her husband immediately took the decision following the fire that the house must be rebuilt.

Amazingly it was achieved in just three years. Over the mantelpiece in the Entrance Hall he had an inscription put up stating (with understandable quiet pride): 'This part of Holker Hall was destroyed by fire March 9 1871 and was rebuilt by William 7 Duke of Devonshire 1874'.

The duke had the resources to rebuild Holker in style. He commissioned the new house from the architectural partnership Paley & Austin of Lancaster, and it was without doubt the grandest country house built in the county at that time. The style chosen was Elizabethan, reflecting the advent of the estate under the family's Preston antecedents, and the emergence of the Cavendish family itself, first in Suffolk and later in Derbyshire. The small, hooded windows associated with Webster's earlier building were replaced by large transom windows on all three floors. There is a swagger to the skyline, only partly hidden behind a balustrade. High pinnacled gables surmount windows that break the roofline, whilst beyond great chimney stacks rear up above the apex of the roof. These are but a prelude to the enormous staircase tower with its pyramid roof topped by jaunty stone balls. If the outline were not enough of a contrast to the earlier building, the colour of it certainly was. Webster's 'Roman cement', a hard and durable plaster, was replaced not by local stone but by stunning red sandstone quarried near Runcorn in Cheshire and brought to Holker by sea. The whole is a triumphal exercise in blending architectural forms from an earlier age.

It could never be mistaken for a sixteenth-century building. It was a majestic bow to the past but Paley & Austin were intent on creating a magnificent contemporary building, using and incorporating the latest technologies, and that is undoubtedly what they achieved. The exterior breathes confidence and durability whilst the inside is redolent of comfort and beauty.

The entrance was placed at what had been the rear of the building, and sufficient space was excavated from the hillside to create a courtyard. Here the main porch, a modified Tudor gateway, is decorated with the duke's coat of arms, surmounted by the Garter which he had been granted in 1838 by a young Queen Victoria. Passing through a small entrance hall, a place to shake off the weather and say goodbye to coats and boots, you enter the Main Hall. Running along the spine of the house and giving access to the main rooms, it comes to a climax in a monumental arcade that brilliantly separates it from the staircase hall. The arcade is made of limestone from the ducal quarries at Staunton near Ulveston. It is cut with faceted panels, those in the upper parts carved with circular patterns. The stone is beautifully polished to glint and gleam in the light, displaying to great advantage the fossil patterns. The walls of the Hall are half-panelled in oak, with carvings in the upper panels of local flora and fauna. In the centre is a great Elizabethan-style stone fireplace, complete with Ionic pilasters decorated with strapwork, its mantelpiece bearing the carved inscription telling of the fire and the rebuilding. To either side are fragments of marble, poignant reminders of the inferno. Some days after the tragedy Lord Frederick Cavendish found a marble pedestal which appeared to have escaped undamaged, but sadly this was illusory. When he tried to move it to a safe location, the whole thing disintegrated. The fragments were gathered up and inserted into the fireplace as a perpetual memorial. On the opposite wall are three great leaded windows which are enhanced with small heraldic stained-glass panels, helping to disguise the view of the courtyard below.

The feeling of warmth and comfort to be found in the Hall extends into the adjacent Library. Bookcases line the walls, but as they rise only to three-quarters of the height of the room they do not overwhelm the space. The sense of relaxed enjoyment is enhanced by the inclusion of two fireplaces, one at either end. Here we find the architects at their most innovative, contrasting cut stone with inset patterns in Italian marble and Derbyshire alabaster. Above each, their craftsmen have created rich 'frames' for the fine pair of portraits of Lord Frederick Cavendish (1836–1882), who alerted the family to the fire, and his wife, the Honourable Lucy Lyttelton, daughter of George, Lord Lyttelton, niece of Gladstone and maid of honour to Queen Victoria. Both these portraits are by Sir William Blake Richmond RA, whose most celebrated contribution to English art is the mosaic in the apse of St Paul's Cathedral. The young woman, shown wearing a white dress offset by black hoops, stands in front of

Opposite: The Main Hall, showing the fireplace containing the inscription and pieces of the shattered marble pedestal, and some of the royal portraits from the Devonshire collection at Bolton Abbey.

an architectural background softened by the delicate oriental plate. The portrait of her husband shows a relaxed, intelligent young man with a luxuriant red beard, lost in thought. It is possible that his beard was to cost him his life. After serving in Gladstone's ministry, Cavendish was sent to Ireland in 1882 as chief secretary under the viceroy, the Earl Spencer. On 6 May, the very day of his installation, he was walking with the under secretary, Mr Burke, in the grounds of the viceroy's house in Dublin when assassins struck and murdered them both. Lord Spencer suspected he, rather than the unknown Cavendish, was the intended target of the assailant's knife, as they both had a luxuriant red beard.

It is in the Library that you encounter another Cavendish ancestor, the distinguished but unsociable Henry Cavendish (1731–1810). Undisturbed by the outside world, he lived chiefly at his house overlooking Clapham Common in London, where he tackled some of the most vexing scientific questions of the day. He discovered nitric acid, studied the properties of the constituents of water – hydrogen and oxygen – and even calculated the density of the earth. The importance of his contribution to scientific progress was lessened, though, by his natural reticence, as he seldom chose to inform others of his discoveries. His fellow scientist Joseph Priestly carried out similar experiments in Birmingham, and whilst he was known to Cavendish (and a copy of Priestley's *History of Electricity* is in the Holker Library), they seldom met.

Cavendish made all encounters difficult. He even had a second staircase constructed in his house purely to avoid meeting his female staff! His interest in the outside world was also strictly limited. This attitude extended even to his own finances, so much so that he inadvertently became one of the largest private investors in the Bank of England. He left his money untouched in his account, accruing interest year on year, and never making contact with the Bank. They even dispatched an emissary to ask what he would like to do with his savings but Cavendish, annoyed by the interruption, replied that if it was causing any trouble, he'd take it away. That was the last time the Bank disturbed him.

On his death, this fortune passed to his cousin once removed, Lord George Augustus Henry Cavendish (1754–1834), who had previously inherited Holker. You might therefore reasonably imagine that Henry Cavendish's microscope, now proudly displayed in the Library, had been in the house since his death but this is not the case. It was more recently acquired by Hugh, the present Lord Cavendish, who is a great admirer of this brilliant and most eccentric of ancestors. Hugh is also justly delighted at having recovered the portrait of William Cavendish, 2nd Earl of Devonshire (1590–1628), which he found in New York. It now hangs in the Dining Room, showing the earl wearing his new peer's robes of scarlet velvet and ermine, devised for the coronation of Charles I.

The Drawing Room forms the first of the enfilade of rooms along the garden front. Here Paley & Austin's naturalistically carved oak panelling rises to the dado, above which the walls are covered in their original Macclesfield silk. The plaster ceiling echoes late-Elizabethan examples whilst the frieze, with its alternating pattern of flowers and rosettes, seems to have been a Paley & Austin invention. The eighteenth century makes an unexpected appearance in the beautiful white marble fireplace, acquired in 1874 by the duke's only daughter, Lady Louisa Egerton, from Montague House in London for £168. Above it the architects created a classically inspired gilt mirror reflecting the light that floods in from the windows on two sides. On the far wall hangs the large *Storm at Sea* by the French artist Claude-Joseph Vernet, commissioned by Holker's eighteenth-century owner Sir William Lowther (1727–1756) when in Rome on his Grand Tour. This was originally one of a pair; its counterpart *Calm at Sea* was a casualty of the 1871 fire, as were so many of the other Old Masters he collected. An amusing picture of Sir William himself survives, in

Opposite: Lord Frederick Cavendish (1836–1882), who was murdered in Dublin, by Sir William Blake Richmond, R.A.

Above: The Hon. Lucy Lyttleton, Lady Frederick Cavendish (1841–1925) by Sir William Blake Richmond, R.A.

a rare caricature painted in Rome by the young Sir Joshua Reynolds. It shows Sir William with his friends Sir Charles Turner and Lord Middleton, and their tutor, Mr Hurst. This is a fine antidote to the typical 'Grand Tour' portraits by Pompeo Batoni and others, where Italian butter wouldn't melt in the young bloods' mouths, and indeed to Reynolds' own fine sensitive portrait of the sitter in the Dining Room.

The central room in the enfilade, now the Billiard Room, has been transformed by Hugh and Grania. The extent of their work can be best seen by comparing photographs in earlier guidebooks. You can hardly believe it is the same room. The pale cream wallpaper and thin red curtains have been replaced by rich hand-stencilled wall coverings, worked in eight layers of paint, William & Morris fabrics and newly releathered tub chairs. The whole scheme reinforces the view of Baudelaire (the nineteenth-century French critic) that nothing is more striking than a combination of red and green – even the table has been refelted to give a perfect green foil for all those red balls that need to be potted. On two sides of the room hang spectacular fowl paintings – exotic chickens and other birds in verdant classical landscapes. It is rare to find such paintings in England. They were painted in Piedmont in the late seventeenth century, and found their way to Holker via Devonshire House in London.

The paintings to the right of the fireplace are a more home-grown affair, showing local views by a local artist painted a few decades later. These charming, somewhat naive paintings are by Matthew Read, a sign painter and topographer much patronized by the Lowther family. The upper view shows Lowther Castle, which became, and remains today the principal seat of the family, now the Earls of Lonsdale. The other painting is more unusual; a rare depiction of an English industrial landscape. It shows the port of Whitehaven, built by the Lowther family on the west coast of the Lake District. Here they created a harbour, sheltered from the winds of the Irish Sea, from where to export coal from their mines all over England. Behind the harbour they arranged for a handsome town to be built, its streets laid out to a grid plan and its houses of local stone and slate. In the centre their classical church sits in a grassy square, reminiscent of the layout of towns across the Atlantic such as New Haven in Connecticut. Ingeniously, the church pulpit was set on rails so that it could be pushed into the centre of the nave for the service and afterwards repositioned to the side. With such enterprise and invention, it is no surprise that the Lowthers made themselves the richest and most influential family in the area during the eighteenth century, and Holker blossomed under their ownership.

Sir William Lowther (c.1660–1704) was a kinsman of John, 1st Viscount Lowther, Lord Privy Seal, and Sir James Lowther, 4th Baronet, Vice Admiral of Cumberland and Clerk of the Ordinance. Like many of his family, Sir William married an heiress. Catherine Preston was the only child of Thomas Preston. Her grandfather had settled his family at Holker at the beginning of the seventeenth century, having purchased the lands from nearby Cartmel Priory at the dissolution of the monasteries. Preston built a fortified peel-tower, part of which survives embedded in the old family wing. Their estates were sequestrated by Parliament during the Civil War, the income channelled into government coffers, but the land was returned at the Restoration.

Sir William and Lady Lowther both died in the early 1700s and were succeeded by their infant son, Sir Thomas Lowther (c.1690–1745). The estate was carefully guarded by his maternal grandmother, and by the time he came to his maturity he was a wealthy young man. Like his father before him, he was Member of Parliament for Lancaster, sitting for the constituency from 1722

Opposite: Sir William Lowther (1727-1756) by Sir Joshua Reynolds PRA.

to 1745. He married the redoubtable Lady Elizabeth Cavendish, daughter to William, 2nd Duke of Devonshire, a link that would bring Holker to the Cavendishes some fifty years later. Sir Thomas and Lady Elizabeth enlarged the house and laid out new formal gardens, enlivened by statues brought by sea from London. No portraits of Sir Thomas have survived though one of his wife now hangs in the Dining Room, showing her dressed in pink shot silk, with her hair cut short – the epitome of fashion in the early eighteenth century. The piece of paper she holds is not a letter, as you would expect, but part of Handel's score for his opera *Tamberlane*. Her interests in the arts were clearly inherited by her only son William, the collector of many of the Old Masters that fell victim to the fire.

Sir William Lowther, who succeeded his father in 1745, was clearly a very cultivated figure and it would be interesting to know more about his Holker. Unfortunately, little of it remains, except at the back of the old wing. Here, if you peer over the wall, you get a glimpse of the eighteenth-century house. It is an interesting mixture of architecture: some windows have thick lintels, others more delicate, and some have very smart hexagonal glazing bars. It is difficult to unpick the dates, though the changing styles reveal that each generation sought to improve the house. It might be that the hexagonal windows were commissioned by Sir William. The Gothick windows at the other end of the building are almost certainly part of the improvements carried out by his cousin and successor, Lord George Augustus Cavendish (c.1727–1794). He commissioned John Carr of York to carry out additions in an 'elegant modern style' between 1783 and 1793. The son of William, 3rd Duke of Devonshire, Lord George inherited Holker in 1756. At that time he was Member of Parliament for the family seat of Derbyshire, a position he would hold until his death. By that time he had become Father of the House of Commons and was known as 'Truth and Daylight', on account of his integrity. You get a sense of that in the portrait painted of him towards the end of his life. What engages the viewer are the piercing blue eyes that look out from his ruddy countenance. He is still taking a lively interest in the world around him. At Holker his work was not confined to the house, but included substantial improvements to the grounds. He swept away the formal gardens laid out by Sir Thomas and Lady Elizabeth, replacing them with parkland – a move which reflects the influence of 'Capability' Brown. Many fine trees were planted, including the majestic cedar grown from seed sent by a friend of his travelling in the Middle East.

It is a feature of Holker that, like the house, its grounds have been subject to continual change, its very location inviting intervention. The area has a warm, temperate climate owing to the influence of the Gulf Stream, but also endures cold winds from the north and east as well as early frosts. Trees have been planted at exposed sites to shelter the gardens to the south and west of the house from the worst of the weather. Little is known of the sixteenth- and seventeenth-century layout, beyond that it would certainly have included

knot gardens, vegetable and herb gardens, and most likely a fenced deer park. With the arrival of the Lowthers, formal gardens were set out with clipped hedges, statuary and swathes of lawn. Again this design fell victim to fashion, replaced by the contrived naturalness laid out by Lord George Augustus, which included walks and even a summer house where the jovial old bachelor would sit with his two brothers, both also bachelors, enjoying the view and a drink of an evening. Whilst trees from this period still populate the parkland, it was to be his eventual successor, William Cavendish, 7th Duke of Devonshire (1808–1891), who laid out the present pleasure grounds. Covering some twenty-two acres, the formality of the early Victorian terrace gardens

gave way to an arboretum established to the north-west. The overall design, which incorporated balustraded terraces, hot houses and a large conservatory, may have been suggested by Sir Joseph Paxton, the 6th Duke of Devonshire's gardener at Chatsworth.

Paxton certainly supplied the seed for the great monkey puzzle tree brought back from Chile by his friend William Holst in 1844. The tree still stands despite having been uprooted during a storm in the 1880s. This provided yet another challenge for the 7th Duke, the tree rising like another phoenix as it was righted by a team of seven shire horses. His son Spencer, 8th Duke of Devonshire, left the estate to his second son, Lord Richard Cavendish (1871–1946), and his wife, Lady Moyra de Vere Beauclerk, daughter of the Duke of St Albans. Lord Richard again set to work transforming the gardens, employing the famous Edwardian garden designer Thomas Mawson. Together they introduced new terraces, walks

and herbaceous borders. The rose garden is the most prominent feature to survive from that time. It is typical of Mawson's architectural approach, with a semi-circle containing a series of beds and geometric walks flanked by two loggias. Roses are planted everywhere, with climbers held aloft by a construction of poles and chains. It is a floral confection in the height of summer, made all the more enjoyable by its sequestered site.

Over the years Paxton's and Mawson's designs have been softened, first by the clever planting of trees and shrubs by Pamela Cavendish, wife of Lord Richard's son, and now by Hugh and Grania themselves. Nothing in nature stays static, especially when it comes to topiary. Grania confesses that one example began life simply as a topiary hedgehog, but over the years it transmuted first into a porcupine and has now metamorphosed into a punk aardvark. The whole garden is rather like that – it keeps developing. When Hugh inherited in 1972 his main preoccupation was simply to try to keep things going. In common with most estates, the Second World War and later high taxation drastically affected their economics. This, combined with periodic outbreaks of dry rot and leaks in the roof, was very dispiriting. But challenges had been met before, and Hugh and Grania are not ones to shrink in the face of such difficulties. To celebrate their initial success in returning the house to a reasonable state, they introduced something brand new: a tinkling water cascade in the heart

Opposite: *Ancient lime tree, originally planted by Sir William Lowther circa 1700.*

Above: *The aardvark in the Topiary Garden.*

of the garden. As Hugh says, it is good to do something positive rather than endlessly tackling problems. Two aspects of the cascade give them particular pleasure: it looks as if it has always been there (they set out to enhance the grounds, rather than to obliterate the work of the past) and the sound and sight of running water brings great enjoyment to their younger visitors. There are surprises and delights in abundance, from formal gardens to wild-flower meadows, planted specimen trees and a monolithic labyrinth, and even a great new sundial devised by Hugh's friend and neighbour Mark Lennox-Boyd. The sundial is made from the largest piece of slate ever to be turned on a lathe, and the calibrations are so accurately placed that the time can be told to within a minute when the sun is shining. It is made entirely of slate from the Burlington slate quarries that Hugh rejuvenated, the success of which has certainly contributed to the restoration of the house and gardens.

Some things are too good to change, one such example being the curved windows

Opposite: *The Cascade created by Lord and Lady Cavendish in the gardens.*

Above: *The vast slate sundial designed by Mark Lennox-Boyd for his friend Hugh Cavendish, looking across the park in winter.*

in the Principal Bedroom. These were originally part of Webster's design of the 1830s, and Paley & Austin produced their own more exciting variant. From the centre of the room you step into the curve of the tower, applied to the south-west corner of the building, and through six double windows can look out across the garden, the trees and into the distant park. This was the 7th Duke's bedroom (and the upper part of the panelling is carved with an abstract design derived from his Christian name, William). His bedroom is kept partly as a memorial to the man whose resolve meant that the house was rebuilt. A reminder of this achievement is the fact that his fireplace is made up around six banisters which were salvaged after the conflagration.

As elsewhere, Grania has here subtly enhanced the Victorian qualities of the interiors. The post-war pale wallpaper has been replaced by one richly patterned in red, picking up details from the patterns on the ceiling. A bolder coloured carpet now lies on the floor, whilst the windows have lost their rather insipid curtains and gained richly patterned green ones (that same love of red and green seen in the Billiard Room). In the adjacent Queen Mary Bedroom (the wife of King George V stayed at Holker in 1937), the faded William Morris

Opposite: *The Duke's Bedroom. Designed by Paley & Austin for William, 7th Duke of Devonshire as part of his rebuilding of the house. His monogrammed name appears in the panelling behind the lamp on the right.*

Below: *The base of the specimen marble table showing sphinx supports.*

chintz has been replaced. The original blocks had survived and so Grania had it reprinted. Another nice touch is the ribbon threaded through the edges of the well-plumped cushions, copied from a nineteenth-century original found in the house. Throughout there is a lightness of touch, even shown when incorporating treasures from other ducal houses, such as the fine eighteenth-century mirrors in the bedrooms (now painted white) and the Devonshire House chandeliers in the Hall. Here they illuminate the royal portraits brought from Bolton Abbey to remedy the deficiencies caused by the fire. These include the stunning portrait of Catherine de Braganza, wife of Charles II, painted by the court artist Jacob Huysman.

The carving to the staircase is another reminder of the brilliance of Paley & Austin's craftsmen. It is wonderfully crisp and entirely inventive, each baluster (of which there are around a hundred) carved to a different design. The genius behind this may be John Crace, the leading decorator of the day, who is known to have been consulted by the architects. He may also be responsible for the stunning table base on the landing that supports a chequerboard of marble specimens. These range from porphyry to lapis and Siena yellow marble. Tables of this type were very popular with English tourists to Italy at the beginning of the nineteenth century. However, the rich mahogany base is clearly from a later date. What a piece of invention: two fabulous sphinxes, half women, half winged lions, their heads and bodies acting as the table's legs and extending down to great paws; their outstretched wings the support for the marble top.

Their tails swish round and their whole bodies are taut and alert. No one knows whether this highly idiosyncratic base replaced one that was destroyed in the fire, but it is pleasant to believe that the sphinxes might have arrived here as the architectural phoenix was arising. The passing of time puts matters into perspective, and looking back to the great fire of 1871, it seems now to be just another phase in the history of this magnificent house. Each generation seems to have responded enthusiastically to Holker's opportunities and challenges, delighted by their good fortune in living here.

Penshurst Place, Kent

The seat of the Viscounts De L'Isle

Previous spread: *a distant view of Penshurst Place in the valley of the Medway.*

Cresting a small hill in the eastern part of Kent, you find yourself looking down into the Medway valley. The sweep of the country is encircled by wooded hills whilst lush meadows follow the course of the river. Here lies Penshurst Place, nestling in the centre looking from this distance more like a village than a house. The building does not follow some formal eighteenth-century plan, nor is it a series of detached buildings clustered round an ancient keep; there is instead an endless variety of roofs, towers, wings and courtyards. The pattern of the buildings is certainly enticing, and equally so are their colours. Penshurst is built in a range of materials, from the palest of stones and stuccoes to the rich yellow-brown of the local ironstone and several shades of brick. The roofs again offer a delicious jumble: pantiles, lead and stone. In the words of the current owner, Philip De L'Isle, it is 'the most delightful mish-mash', reflecting the fact that no one in his family, the Sidneys, has been bold enough (or rich enough) to start again from scratch. Penshurst is a house that has grown like Topsy; almost every generation has added or subtracted something, leaving a building whose geography confounds all first time visitors.

Beyond the house you can see the gardens, the closest being formally laid out and thereafter a series of long beds and orchards, with well-tended vegetable beds screened by hedges. The land to the south is bordered by a high wall that drops steeply down to a lane leading to the parish church and the village of Penshurst. This is a particularly English scene: a grand country house sitting peacefully in the surrounding landscape, looking much as it has done for centuries. In the sixteenth century Penshurst Place (already then more than 200 years old) was given to Philip's ancestors by a grateful Edward VI. The architecture and aspirations of both its earliest owners and successive members of the Sidney family can still be discerned today.

In 1552 Edward VI presented this estate to his loyal servant Sir William Sidney. The family had been landowners in Surrey and Sussex in the fifteenth century, and William had decided to try his luck at the early-Tudor court under the patronage of his uncle, Sir Thomas Brandon. He fared well in the jostling for position, serving with military distinction at the battle of Flodden Field, and acting as a proficient courtier under Henry VIII. He was appointed Chamberlain to the newly born Prince Edward in 1538, and rose to become steward of his household six years later. Penshurst was his reward for the dedication and loyalty he had shown. Sadly, he did not live long to enjoy it, dying just two years after the gift was made.

William's son and heir, Henry Sidney, had been the childhood companion of Prince Edward, so not surprisingly he became a central figure at the young king's court. He married Mary Dudley, daughter of the Duke of Northumberland – the most powerful courtier of the day – and in so doing allied himself to the Protestant faction. When Edward VI died unexpectedly in 1553, expiring in his arms, Henry found himself aligned with those supporters of Lady Jane Grey's claim to the throne. Wisely he managed to distance himself to see how matters developed, but not before seeing his Dudley relations felled by the executioner's axe. Henry himself had to seek Queen Mary's pardon, which she gave together with her confirmation that the estate of Penshurst was given to his family in perpetuity.

Approaching Penshurst today, the first tall building you encounter is the King's Tower, erected by Sir Henry Sidney in 1585 to commemorate the royal gift. This stone tower (replacing an earlier fourteenth-century one) dominates the north front, rising high above the flanking building and jutting out from the wall line. In the centre, above a crisp classical gateway, sits the royal arms of Edward VI. Higher up a handsome tablet incorporated into the wall bears a long inscription recording the munificent gift by 'the most Religious and renown Prince Edward the Sixt'. It is when you pass through the double doors of the tower and enter the courtyard, you become aware of the scale of that gift. By Tudor standards the house was already large. It had been the seat of two royal dukes in the fifteenth century, and home to the most influential nobleman in the land at the turn of the sixteenth. There are two great halls and a succession of interconnecting buildings, all designed in the most sophisticated styles of the day. The Sidneys had no need to build (unlike the Cecils at Burghley), instead confining themselves to slowly adapting the building to suit their tastes. This has meant that behind the great tower at Penshurst is one of the most intact buildings to have survived from late medieval times.

Of the very earliest house on this site, which dated from the thirteenth century, nothing remains save for a memorial to its creator, Sir Stephen de Penchester, at the parish church. The original building was probably rather modest in scale, as Sir Stephen preferred to live at his substantial castle at Allington, near

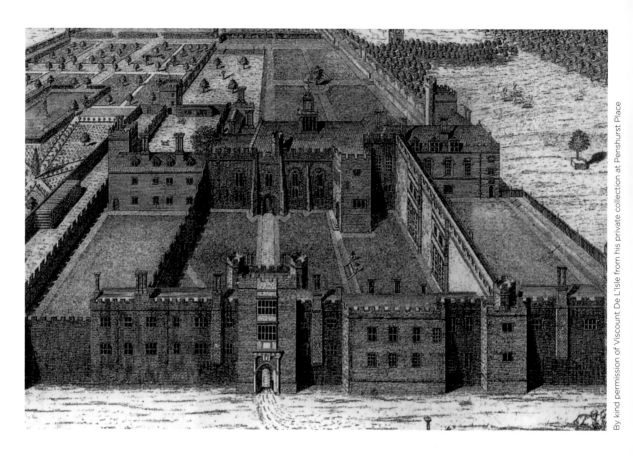

By kind permission of Viscount De L'Isle from his private collection at Penshurst Place

Above: *A prospective view of Penshurst showing the King's Tower in the foreground from a print after George Vertue.*

Opposite: *The Baron's Hall looking towards the screen with the open hearth at its centre.*

Maidstone. Whatever its size, it seems likely to have been pulled down by Sir John de Pulteney, a city magnate who acquired the lands from Sir Stephen's descendants in 1338. During the next decade, Penshurst's new owner built an unusually grand courtyard house, centred on a spectacular Baron's Hall. This is constructed from irregularly cut blocks of local sandstone, their yellow colour streaked with the brownish stains of iron. The varying sizes and colours coupled with the oddness of the coursing gives an engaging patchwork quality to the external walls. You enter through a porch now surmounted by the Sidney arms and topped with their porcupine. (Philip intimates that the family had a reputation for being rather prickly, and if so, this has done them no harm!) Passing under a vaulted passage you arrive at the fourteenth-century door, with a handy internal wicket for daily use. You realize how much shorter medieval man must have been as you duck beneath the portal to pass along a screened passage with doors that lead to the Kitchen, Buttery and Pantry, before entering the hall itself.

Nothing on the outside, even the high roofline, prepares you for the scale of the hall's interior. The room measures a staggering 62 by 32 feet, and rises some 60 feet high. It is flooded with light from a series of Gothic windows set along both sides – an emphatic display of Pulteney's wealth, given that glass was extremely expensive. Everything here was built to impress – and this building still does. The scale is enhanced by the paleness of the walls and the beauty of the great roof. This is built of chestnut (a lighter wood than the oak more typically found

in such buildings) and it carries the huge span through a system of collared beams and king posts. This is thought to be the work of the royal carpenter, William Hurley. The internal tensions are carefully held in balance – the thrust of its weight and that of the stone roof above is cleverly directed outwards to where the windows are surrounded by large arches, and the walls are supported by stout buttresses, the large blocks of local stone serving the purpose well.

Originally the room would have been a riot of colour, but now the walls are washed with white and the woodwork has bleached. Even the carved figures that stand along the roofline have lost their paintwork, appearing like ghostly apparitions from Chaucer's *Canterbury Tales*. Colour now comes from the rich roof timbers and the reddish-pink baked tiles on

A wooden figure from the roofline of the Baron's Hall.

the floor below. These cover the entire space, rising to a dais at the far end. In the centre stands the original hearth, edged with pale stone, where great logs still blaze atop the large Gothic trivet on cold days. This is undoubtedly one of the greatest interiors to have survived from the Middle Ages, dating around forty years earlier than Westminster Hall, and it still resonates loudly with the power and deep pockets of its builder, Sir John de Pulteney.

Pulteney was one of the leading London merchants of his day and, like the fictional Dick Whittington, he rose to become Lord Mayor. He established his initial fortune as a member of the Draper's Company and thereafter became one of the chief financiers supporting the royal coffers and campaigns of the young Edward III. At the time he acquired Penshurst Pulteney already owned two town houses in London and a number of landed properties throughout southern England. His new estate was well placed, lying between the capital and the trading ports along the south-east coast. He was deeply entrenched in business there and after the capture of Calais in 1347 he was one of the merchants to be dispatched by Edward III to that highly important commercial town, charged with advising on its administration. Penshurst would seem to have provided him with a place to relax and enjoy the fruits of his labours. Certainly the records show it was used for hunting, with warrens for hares, rabbits, pheasant, partridge and herons. The Baron's Hall was his banqueting house, used to entertain friends and potential clients. But these days of magnificence were cut short when Pulteney succumbed to the Black Death in 1349.

During the late Middle Ages the estate passed first by inheritance to Sir John Devereux, and then by sale to the Crown. Devereux probably added the regular group of towers that once surrounded the building, but now only the stump of one, the Garden Tower, remains. The first royal occupant was the Duke of Bedford (1389–1435), the younger brother of Henry V. He was both Protector of England, during Henry VI's minority, and Regent of France. Although he owned the estate for only the last five years of his life, he is likely to have built the second Great Hall that sits obliquely to Pulteney's building. This was much altered in the sixteenth century, but the gables are still decorated with his emblems, the falcon and ibex. He also added the impressive late-Gothic staircase to connect the Great Halls. This is a particularly sensitive addition to the earlier building, its wide stone steps spiralling upwards to the first floor lit by a series of carefully placed windows.

The duke was succeeded by his younger brother Humphrey, Duke of Gloucester – a great patron of literature whose books now form part of the Bodleian Library, Oxford. Although he was a notable builder elsewhere, he seems to have limited himself at Penshurst to keeping the buildings in good repair. On his death in 1447 the estate was given by Henry VI to another Humphrey; Humphrey Stafford, 1st Duke of Buckingham. It remained in his family until the 3rd Duke was executed in 1522 by Henry VIII for 'presumption'. His royal ancestry got the better of his judgement at the Field of the Cloth of Gold, where his lavish display and use of the royal arms proved too much for the king. Thereafter Penshurst reverted to the Crown, until granted to the Sidneys some thirty years later.

The late-sixteenth-century members of the Sidney family emerge not so much through Penshurst, their newly acquired building, but in the portraits hanging throughout the house. They are among a remarkable collection of early English portraits – one of the best in the country. Hanging in the Long Gallery, near to a portrait of Edward VI from the studio of William Scrots, is the forceful painting of Sir Henry Sidney. Sir Henry stands erect, smartly but quietly attired in a dark doublet and hose with a short cape. This is a man of moderation and fortitude; keeping his life in balance between the extremes hinted at to either side – the disciplined classical ornament to the left and the frenzy of drapery to the right. After securing the estate under Queen Mary, Sir Henry remained in royal service under Elizabeth I, closely tied to the fortune of his cousin Robert Dudley, Earl of Leicester – the queen's favourite. His royal duties meant that he was often absent from Kent, either in Ireland, where he acted as the queen's deputy in the 1560s and 70s, or at Ludlow Castle in Shropshire, as president of the Council of Wales. When able, and as his financial resources allowed, he improved the buildings at Penshurst, building the King's Tower in 1585, replacing the screen in the Great Hall and probably adding the classical loggia that now forms the outer wall to the Library. His initials, entwined with those of his wife Mary, are inscribed on the water hoppers in the internal courtyard.

Alongside these portraits hangs that of Sir Henry's eldest son, Sir Philip Sidney, who was born at Penshurst in 1554. He was adroitly christened after Queen Mary's husband, Philip of Spain, and spent his early years in Kent. He grew up to become one of the most celebrated, and certainly one of the most cultivated, figures of the age. A poet, man of letters, diplomat and soldier, he helped to shape the late-Elizabethan era through his writings and his chivalry. The court revolved around the queen, his 'Gloriana', whom he celebrated in verse:

> *Like sparkling gems her virtues draw the sight*
> *And in her conduct she is always bright.*
> *When she imparts her thoughts, her words have force,*
> *And sense and wisdom flow in sweet discourse.*

Who could remain unmoved by such flattering lines? His portrait shows a handsome young man who has inherited his father's looks and auburn hair. Fashion

Opposite: *Sir Philip Sidney (1554–1586) by an unknown artist.*

Below: *The anonymous painting called* Queen Elizabeth Dancing with Robert Dudley, Earl of Leicester.

has moved on, and the son wears an elaborate lace ruff above a tight-fitting slashed doublet with more lace to the cuffs. His pantaloons balloon out and are stitched with fine thread, whilst around his shoulders he wears damascene armour, the metal inlaid with gold wire in imitation of the decorative cloth and metalwork made in that city.

Like his father, Sir Philip was right at the centre of court life and a glimpse of that world and its intrigues may be caught in another painting at Penshurst. This shows the interior of a large room, lit by lamps, with musicians playing and two elegant figures dancing in the centre. Long known as *Queen Elizabeth Dancing with Robert Dudley, Earl of Leicester*, the central male does indeed have a likeness to portraits of Sir Philip's uncle. He is shown supporting the lady with his knee as she leaps into the air – a fancy step from one of the queen's favourite dances, La Volta. Surrounding the central pair are the ladies of the court, the married women wearing high ruffs, the others with open collars, following the dictates of the queen. The musicians on the left are playing various stringed instruments, and they too have been identified. The figure in the foreground playing the large bass viol is thought to be Queen Elizabeth's Bolognese composer and viol player Alfonso Frescobaldi; the violinists are likely to be Richard Tarrant and Caesar Galliardello. In the lower right corner another prominent figure is shown with his back towards us – a young gentleman, smartly dressed although wearing his plumed hat in the queen's presence and almost certainly with his arm around the waist of the pretty girl next to him. He has been identified as Elizabeth's French suitor, Charles Duc D'Alençon, whilst the bearded figure of a second gentleman, bending his head, is said to be Sir Philip Sidney himself. If these identifications are correct, then the painting is of something more significant than mere court entertainment. Opinions are divided, and much revolves around who commissioned it. It may have been painted in France for the critics of Charles, who came to England around 1580 to woo the queen but failed both to dislodge Leicester from her favours (or apparently to cease his own philandering). However, if painted for the English, it is argued that it shows Leicester in his rightful position as principal courtier, bowed to by his cousin Sir Philip, whilst the perfidious Frenchman dallies elsewhere.

What is certain is that Sir Philip was seen as one of the great ornaments of the court. A favourite of the queen and, from 1583, son-in-law of her minister Sir Francis Walsingham, he was set to rise; but events overtook expectations. In 1586 he took part in the military expedition to the Spanish Netherlands and was mortally wounded at the battle of Zutphen. The queen and the court went into deep mourning, and he was afforded a state funeral – an honour bestowed outside the royal family only twice since, to the Duke of Wellington and Sir Winston Churchill. A poignant reminder of that event stands in the Armoury at Penshurst – the metal porcupine crested helm that was carried before the bier on its slow and solemn passage to the funeral rites in the old St Paul's Cathedral.

Sir Philip died just months after his father, and Penshurst then passed to his younger brother, Robert, and his amiable Welsh wife, Barbara Gamage. She was not only amiable but also rich. Her father, John Gamage of Coity in Glamorgan, accrued a fortune so substantial that on his death in 1584 there was a scramble to secure the hand of his only daughter and heir. Even the queen was involved, sending out instructions that no one could marry Mistress Gamage without royal

Opposite: *Sir Philip Sidney's helm with porcupine crest carried at his state funeral.*

Above: *A herald carrying Sir Philip Sidney's helm at his state funeral.*

Above: Barbara Gamage, Lady Sidney later Countess of Leicester with her elder children by Marcus Gheeraerdts the Younger.

Opposite: The State Dining Room, created in the late 16th century out of the medieval Solar.

consent. Walsingham and Lord Pembroke leaked this information to Sir Henry Sidney, who as Lord President of Wales was well aware of the opportunity and who wished to secure the lady for his younger son. He achieved his aim and the young couple were wed before the messenger arrived with the queen's orders.

Theirs was a happy marriage, Lady Sidney accompanying her husband to Flushing (Vlissingen) in the Netherlands, where Robert was governor for most of the 1590s. When they had to be apart, he wrote touching letters asking of her welfare that still survive. She appears in a near-life-size portrait by Marcus Gheeraerdts that hangs in the State Dining Room, surrounded by five of her eleven children. This is a work of enormous charm, the children dressed in embroidered cream clothes and all with the flame-red hair of the Sidneys. The artist, whose family came from Bruges, was one of a number of painters from the Low Countries who worked in England during the second half of the sixteenth century. Here you witness a loosening of the strict formality of earlier English portraiture. In the centre stands the eldest son holding a velvet cap, a sword at his side although he is yet to be breached and still wears a skirt. His younger brother perches on a table, his dangling legs obscured by an apron. He holds a coral rattle in one hand and two fat cherries in the other. The two younger girls are identically dressed,

whilst the eldest daughter on the right is more elaborately decked out. The daughter closest to her mother is Mary, later Lady Mary Roth, who would write *Urania*, the first romance ever to be penned by an English woman. Large family portraits involving so many figures were uncommon in England at the time and this commission probably reflects the fact that Lady Sidney was unusually close to her children. She took them with her when she visited her husband in the Netherlands, and kept her eldest son at home long beyond the point at which her husband considered he should have been sent to a tutor.

The political fortunes of the Sidney family improved immeasurably on the accession of James I. Largely unrewarded by Queen Elizabeth, Robert skilfully steered a course through the rebellion of the Earl of Essex. When James I took the crown, Robert was ennobled as Lord Sidney of Penshurst and soon made Lord Chamberlain of Queen Anne of Denmark's household and Surveyor of her

Revenues. He was raised in 1605 to Viscount Lisle, again in 1616 to Knight of the Garter and finally, in 1618, achieved his long-standing ambition when James I revived his uncle's former title, creating him Earl of Leicester. The rise in his fortunes – financial as well as political – encouraged him to commission portraits, acquiring fine works of art and undertaking new building. The inventory taken on his death in 1623 reveals the lavishness of his wardrobe and of the furnishing of his houses. Although his income had increased, it is perhaps not surprising to learn that his expenditure outstripped it, often leaving him in a perilous financial state. He wrote to his wife: 'If my ill-wishers should know what state I am in, it was a subject enough for them to laugh at me for ever'. From this historical distance you cannot help but be grateful for his extravagance, as not only do his splendid paintings line the walls of the State Dining Room but also the rooms he added to Penshurst include one of the most splendid.

In the early years of the seventeenth century he added a wing to the house, linking the remodelled second Great Hall to one of Sir John Devereux's remaining towers. On the upper floor he created a beautifully proportioned Long Gallery, lit by a succession of large windows on three sides that afforded views over his elaborate formal gardens. The room is panelled throughout with a complex interplay of shapes enlivened by ornaments placed at regular intervals and separated by fluted columns. At the column bases pendant shapes hang above inset lozenges, whilst tightly scrolled Ionic capitals cap the tops. The frieze around the room is equally inventive, having a play of pendant half-bosses alternating with ribbed triglyths. This is work of great sophistication and delight – every inch carefully considered by a master craftsman and made with great accuracy by a skilled carpenter. It is rather surprising that its proportions were destroyed in the eighteenth century, when the floor level was lowered to match that in the adjacent Tapestry Room. Fortunately, in 1921, Philip's great-uncle took advantage of an outbreak of dry rot to remedy this, also taking the opportunity to add a fine plasterwork ceiling incorporating elements of the Sidney crest. The process of sensitive restoration to these early rooms began in the nineteenth century. The measured programme continues today responding to the very individual character of the different rooms created over the last 700 years.

Opposite: The Long Gallery created for the 1st Earl of Leicester at the beginning of the 17th century. In the foreground, the Italian 18th-century inlaid table by Gori with the family armorials commissioned by William Perry.

It was Robert (the young boy perched on the table in the large family portrait) who inherited the estate, becoming 2nd Earl of Leicester in 1626 (his older brother William having died before their father). Robert Sidney had been educated at Oxford and then as a lawyer before following the family tradition of royal service. In 1632 Charles I appointed him as ambassador to his uncle, Charles IV of Denmark, and Robert sailed to Copenhagen. There he found life in the Danish court was unlike that in the English one he was accustomed to. Charles I and Henrietta Maria lived an elegant, dignified life, whilst Robert wrote that the Danish King 'lived a strange life . . . drunk every day, lying with a whore every night'. However, he managed to hold his own and later noted proudly that, following the feast given in his honour at the end of his embassy, which commenced

at eleven in the morning and lasted well into the night, he was able to climb the stairs unaided – unlike the king, who was carried up on a chair!

After his appointment to Denmark came France, where he was sent in 1636 as Charles I's ambassador to his brother-in-law, Louis XIII. He remained there until 1641, dealing with his compatriot Lord Scudamore and coping with the court intrigues surrounding the king, Marie de Medici and Cardinal Richelieu (intrigues that would be put to use by Alexander Dumas in *The Three Musketeers*). It may be that the group portrait showing Lord Leicester's three eldest sons, Henry, Algernon, and Robert, that now hangs in the Long Gallery was painted in France. His children certainly accompanied him there, and no satisfactory English attribution has yet been found for the painting.

Robert's return from his diplomatic missions coincided with the political deterioration that led ultimately to the Civil War. He was one of those noblemen who simply could not decide which side to align himself with. Though by temperament a natural supporter of the Crown, he found himself frequently at odds with the king. Yet the Parliamentary cause had very little attraction for him either. In the event he quitted the king at Oxford in 1644, made peace with Parliament and returned to Penshurst. He was shortly afterwards joined by his daughter, Dorothy. Her beauty had turned the head of the poet Edmund Waller, who called her his Sacharissa, 'The beam of beauty, which began / To warm us so, when thou was here'. Her husband, Henry Spencer, 1st Earl of Sunderland, had been killed at the battle of Newbury, where he had fought for the king, whilst her elder brothers, Philip and Algernon, supported Parliament. The English Civil War tore such families apart, and only the most ardent Royalists and committed Parliamentarians found it easy to choose sides.

The peaceful seclusion of Penshurst was temporarily disturbed at the end of that decade, with the arrival of the two youngest royal children, the Duke of Gloucester and the Princess Mary. They arrived in the summer of 1649 following their father's execution, and remained there under the protection of Lady Leicester until her death the following August. Her husband then announced himself as at the point of death, but he in fact survived until 1677. He was at loggerheads with his eldest son and constantly concerned with the well-being of his second, Algernon, whose republican sympathies finally led to his execution on Tower Hill in 1683. The career of Robert's youngest son, Henry (1641–1704), was altogether more fortunate. 'The handsomest youth of his time' was caught by Sir Peter Lely in one of his most enchanting Arcadian portraits, dating from the later 1640s. Lely had trained in Haarlem before coming to England and by 1647 he was employed by the Duke of Northumberland (Lady Leicester's brother, a connection that probably brought him into the Penshurst ambit). Lely's early refined style is seen here at its best – a typically English approach to portraiture forged through his study of Van Dyck and Dobson.

Opposite: Henry Sidney, later Earl of Romney (1641–1704) by Sir Peter Lely.

Henry Sidney grew up at Penshurst, leaving for his continental tour before gravitating in due course to the court of Charles II, where an intimacy with the king's sister-in-law, Anne Hyde, got him into trouble. In 1678 he went to Holland, forming such a good friendship with William, Prince of Orange, nephew to Charles II, that the king saw the benefit of making Henry an Envoy Extraordinary. In time Henry would help to pave the way for the Glorious Revolution, arriving with William at Torbay in 1688 and being created Viscount Sidney at the coronation the following April. In the Tapestry Room at Penshurst stands a spectacular royal gift – an ebony cabinet set with small panels, many by artists working in Utrecht in the mid seventeenth century, and in the centre a sea piece by another contemporary, Bonaventura Peeters from Antwerp. The exterior of the cabinet is further ornamented with a series of well-chased silver-gilt statues set into niches. The central part opens to reveal further silverwork inside: delicately modelled

Above: *A 17th-century Dutch ebony cabinet set with pictures and silver figures, presented to Lord Romney by William III.*

Opposite: *The Queen Elizabeth Room with some of the gilded furniture commissioned by Lord Leicester for Leicester House, London.*

plaques depicting scenes from the New Testament, and in the middle a bust of Christ above a panel of the Nativity. This opens again, revealing an architectural interior, mirrored on all sides and with a pendant cherub. This piece of furniture was given to Henry Sidney by William III, whom he continued to serve as secretary of state for the north, and later as lord lieutenant in Ireland. In 1694 he was created Earl of Romney, and in his later years he lived at the Queen's House at Greenwich. He died in 1704, leaving the estate to his nephew, John Sidney, who would become 6th Earl of Leicester on his brother's death the following year.

During the later seventeenth century the family house in London was close to Leicester Square – the landmark that bears their name. That house eventually proved so costly to maintain that it was intermittently let, mainly to members of the royal family. These running costs included large payments for decoration and refurbishment, and the quality of the furniture can be gauged by the suite of chairs now in the Queen Elizabeth Room at Penshurst. This is English baroque furniture at its grandest; architectural in form, its elaborately carved woodwork applied with burnished gold leaf and the richness of its fabrics set off by tassels

and fringes. The day bed is particularly impressive, with an enormous carved shell at its head. Few pieces of such quality have survived so intact and in such a good state. This suite was undoubtedly made for Leicester House, and probably supplied between 1698 and 1700 when invoices show the 4th Earl spending the then considerable sum of £1,500 on new furniture.

On the walls in this room hangs the group portrait of the earl's granddaughter, Elizabeth Sidney, who inherited Penshurst in 1743. The family line had shrunk to such an extent that only three daughters were born to the 4th Earl's four sons, and thus the Leicester title became extinct. Elizabeth married a wealthy parvenu, William Perry, and you sense that his wife's inheritance went to his head. Plumb in the centre of this painting by David Luders sits Perry and his wife, with their children and pets orbiting them. The canvas contains numerous references to her illustrious family, with painted busts of her Sidney and Dudley antecedents and a view of Penshurst seen through the arcade. Perry was not content with just this frothy rococo portrait by a rather obscure German painter, and to celebrate his new position as 'head' of the Sidney family he went on to fill the house with

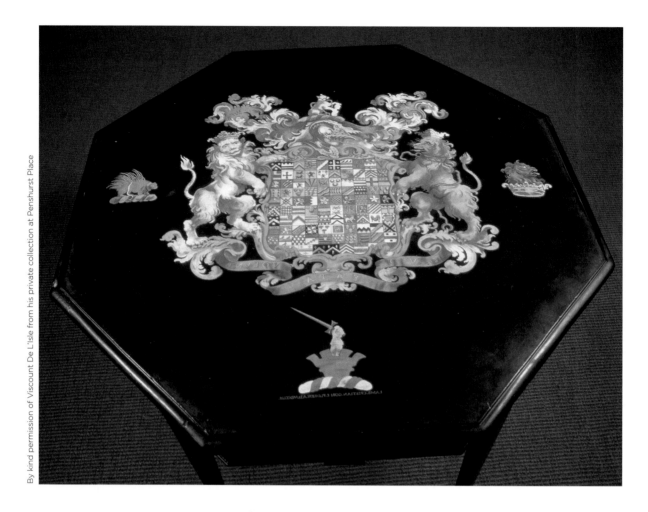

Above: *The Pietra Dura table top by Signor Gori showing an elaboration of the family arms.*

Opposite top: *17th-century painted harpsichord on an elaborate 18th-century giltwood stand, made in Rome and acquired by William Perry.*

Opposite bottom: *Robert Rattray's rearing porcupine, commissioned to celebrate the millenium.*

trophies of his taste. He went on a Grand Tour, returning laden with gilded and marble objects. One of the more outrageous acquisitions is the impressive tabletop made in the ducal workshops in Florence. Perry employed the skills of Signor Gori in a celebration of his 'noble' lineage. In the centre, between his wife's family emblems of a porcupine for Sidney and the bear and ragged staff of Dudley, is a colossal coat of arms with a fantastic number of quarterings to reflect Perry's connections to so many armigerous families. Either by design or misunderstanding, many of these are fanciful – you suspect Perry would not have been unduly concerned.

In many ways, Perry is a delight. There is something irrepressible about him, and his taste has a flamboyance that you cannot help but admire, even if at the time his family and neighbours might have sniggered behind his back. Who else would have bought such a base for the delicate seventeenth-century harpsichord, which is now supported on swirls of Roman gilded woodwork with a frolicking putto pausing to listen to the sound! It was Perry who lowered the floor in the Long Gallery, and who added the tripartite Venetian window at its end. It was not his only window – Perry took the view that the house would be improved by the addition of sash windows throughout. His energy, often misplaced, had such a profound effect on the house that it comes as a surprise to learn he died aged only 47 (sadly spending his latter years in Bedlam, having finally lost his mind).

His widow outlived her husband by twenty-six years, and after her death the estate was put in trust for their young grandson, Sir John Shelley-Sidney (1771–1827). This is the nadir of the estate; in 1808 one Herr Amsinck wrote that 'the mansion is now deserted; and will probably before another generation passes be known only as a ruin'. He had not reckoned with the enterprise of Sir John, who employed J. B. Rebecca to restore the house, creating a new set of family rooms in the Gothick style. These are a delight, a series of late-Regency rooms – Entrance Hall, Dining Room and Drawing Room – running off a vaulted corridor. The first of these is dominated by a magnificent portrait of King William IV whose daughter by Mrs Jordan, Lady Sophia FitzClarence, married Sir John's son Philip. After military service Philip became an equerry to his royal father-in-law, who created him Baron

By kind permission of Viscount De L'Isle from his private collection at Penshurst Place

De L'Isle and Dudley of Penshurst in 1835. This title is still held by the family although when the present owner's father was created a viscount in 1956 he decided to drop 'and Dudley'. He had found this led to some confusion, with two place settings being laid for him at dinners!

The 'improvements' undertaken by Perry were removed during the nineteenth century, when George Devey was commissioned to restore the building. He took great pains with this undertaking, even marking every stone in the wall of the second Great Hall when it was taken down so he could put each one back in its original location when rebuilt. Since then the building has been carefully maintained, latterly by the present owners, Philip, 2nd Viscount De L'Isle, and his wife, Isobel – a process that has no end. During 2005 a series of rooms on the north front was reconfigured as a double office for Philip and Isobel, whilst their son and daughter found niches for themselves elsewhere. Not all this work is purely practical. An occasional rush of blood to the head is permitted. Standing amongst the ancient gardens is an old friend reincarnated. To mark the new millennium, a huge metal porcupine was commissioned, standing proud on his hind legs and surveying the scene. The 1st Lord Leicester, and indeed William Perry, would have been proud!

By kind permission of Viscount De L'Isle from his private collection at Penshurst Place

Scampston Hall, Yorkshire

The seat of Sir Charles Legard, Bt.

Some country houses hide, either behind high walls or in the depths of their parks – Scampston is not one of them. Others appear as if they have grown quite naturally out of their local surroundings – Scampston is not like that either. It is instead a series of surprises, perhaps none so great as the moment when you first encounter it from the road between Malton and Scarborough. The countryside is uneventful, with long views across regular fields, but when you get beyond Rillington you are initially surprised to find that the view is curtailed by plantations of trees. Then it opens up and something magical has happened – it is as if you have returned to the eighteenth century as you pass a beautifully landscaped park, crossing over a balustraded bridge with water to either side, and with a Gothic folly to your right. Then, just as suddenly, this landscape disappears as a closing curtain of further trees returns you once again to the former view. During these moments you may also have caught sight of Scampston itself. Even from here you can see this is one of the most striking and elegant neoclassical houses in the county. The pleasing austerity of its principal façade is a foil to its two great bows, one topped with a monumental dome. In this part of England, houses had to stand their ground against strong neighbourly competition. Although relatively small by some standards, Scampston has no trouble in holding its own, even in a district that includes both the baroque splendours of Castle Howard and the refined beauty of Sledmere.

In the eighteenth century Scampston belonged to the St Quintin family; three generations of them, all called William. Sir William St Quintin, 4th Bt. (1700–1770) came into the estate in the early part of the century. He was succeeded by his son, Sir William 5th Bt., and he in turn by his nephew, William Thomas Darby St Quintin. The current owner, Sir Charles Legard, is the latter's great-great-great-grandson, the house having passed in the female line to

his mother, Mary, who married Sir Thomas Legard of neighbouring Ganton in 1935. Walking through the house with Charles and Caroline, his wife, you keep bumping into his St Quintin and Legard forebears. In the Entrance Hall above the fireplace hangs Gainsborough's portrait of the 4th Baronet; the first of the St Quintins to live here. He is shown toward the end of his life, happy and relaxed as if taking a quiet look at you. His wig is carefully arranged and powdered, his well-brushed black hat held in his hands; there is a sense that all is as it should

be. His air is of well-bred informality, a characteristic shared by his descendants that reappears in Julian Barrow's delightful portrait of Charles's mother, seated at her desk, and that of Charles himself, in a favourite sweater, painted by Andrew Festing. This informality goes with the energy and enterprise that first went into creating the house and estate, and that bubbles up in the present generation.

The St Quintin family came to England from France in the wake of the Norman conquest. By the thirteenth century they were settled at Harpham in the East Riding, between Driffield and the port of Bridlington. The earliest of their family portraits dating from the sixteenth cenury were painted in the Low Countries – Holland being more accessible from Yorkshire than London, and also providing more accomplished painters. The baronetcy was given to William St Quintin (1579–1649) by Charles I at the onset of the Civil War and it was his great-grandson, Sir William, 3rd Bt. (1661–1723), who significantly increased the family's fortunes and position. His portrait, painted by Sir Godfrey Kneller, now hangs in the Dining Room.

In 1695, he was elected Member of Parliament for the most important seat in the county after York – representing the prosperous port of Kingston-upon-Hull. He not only held that seat for eleven successive parliaments, but also secured a series of financially lucrative government appointments. Between 1698 and 1701 he was a Commissioner for Customs, and from 1706 to 1710 Commissioner for Revenue in Ireland. These two roles provided him with an annual salary of £1,000, and his competence led to his appointment as a Lord of the Treasury. He prospered there under Sir Robert Walpole, which must account for the Walpole portraits by Charles Phillips that remain at Scampston today. But Sir William St Quintin's most financially rewarding position was still to come. In June 1720 he was made joint vice-treasurer, receiver general and paymaster of Ireland, a position he held until his death three years later. He died unmarried and the title and his fortune passed to his fortunate nephew, William.

Opposite: Sir William St Quintin 3rd Bt. (1661-1723), Receiver-General and Paymaster of Ireland by Sir Godfrey Kneller Bt.

William was doubly blessed as he also inherited Scampston through his Aunt Mary, who had married James Hustler in 1707. The Hustler family had acquired the estate in the early seventeenth century when William Hustler, a prosperous draper from Bridlington, bought land in the area. It was probably his grandson who built here after the Restoration in 1660. His house became Sir William St Quintin's by the early 1730s and would survive largely unaltered until the end of that century. It was built primarily of brick (stone being a scarce and expensive commodity in the Derwent valley), and if you venture around the back of the present house you can still see the original seventeenth-century brick walls. The Carolean house at Scampston had nine bays looking west, the central bay and those either end projecting forward. It had a steeply hipped roof and the service wing ran off to the north, looking across a courtyard to the stables. In the second half of the eighteenth century William Marlow was commissioned to paint views of the estate and his prospect of the house shows how little it had changed,

save that at some point the red bricks have given way to white painted stucco – a sign of changing fashion.

The young William St Quintin, only 23 when he came into his inheritance, married Rebecca Thompson. His uncle would no doubt have been greatly pleased by the financial prudence of his match, as his wife was the daughter of an exceedingly wealthy London merchant, Sir John Thompson. The security of their financial position meant they could enjoy their estate to the full, indulging their passion for gardening and horse racing – passions that still prevail in the family today. Charles Bridgeman, the leading contemporary gardener, was called on to produce designs for new formal gardens. Although not a trace of his work survives, a drawing in the Bodleian Library in Oxford shows the extent of the St Quintins' ambition. To the west of the house an axial arrangement of clipped trees was envisaged, with areas devoted to formal planting of flowering shrubs, grass walks and a T-shaped canal ending in a large octagonal pool. The whole was to be surrounded by a double row of trees on terraces, and at the far end with an embankment to hide the 'Road from Scarboro' to York'. The entrance front of the house may well have been altered at that time to enable the new gardens to be better appreciated. Certainly in Bridgeman's plan a courtyard is shown to the rear of the house, with the entrance door going into what is now the back of the Staircase Hall.

There is better evidence for Sir William's activities as a breeder of racehorses. He owned the Harpham Arabian (named after his original family house) and Salome, the dam of Scampston Cade and Cypron. The latter 'and her brood' are depicted in the fine painting by Sawrey Gilpin, R.A., which hangs in the Dining Room. This painting came to Scampston through an act of charming generosity from someone who has otherwise historically gained a rather poor reputation. The Duke of Cumberland, George III's uncle and the victor of the battle of Culloden, bought the mare Cypron in 1758 when Sir William advertised his stud for sale. She had already produced notable winners in Dumplin and Dapper, and would go on to foal Herod, who ran extremely successfully for the duke. Seven years later Cumberland commissioned Gilpin to paint his favourite brood mare with her offspring in the shade of a spreading oak tree. To their left, the ducal grooms are seen exercising two racehorses and on the left, 'flying' across the horizon, are three of her winning brood including Dumplin and Dapper. The picture was exhibited at the Royal Academy and entered the Royal Collection. The duke then asked Gilpin to repeat his commission and gave the copy to Sir William as a token of his esteem.

The fine arts seem slowly to have replaced Sir William's earlier interests, especially in the years following Lady St Quintin's death in 1757. In the Morning Room, often used today by Caroline as her study, the walls are thickly hung with landscapes by Richard Wilson, Samuel Scott and Edmund Garvey – all early contributors to the fledgling Royal Academy. Sir William chose well; the Wilson landscapes of Italy are particularly good examples of his classical style

Opposite: *Scampston Hall by William Marlow R.A. circa 1770.*

Below: *Cypron and her brood by Sawrey Gilpin R.A., presented to Sir William St Quintin by the Duke of Cumberland.*

BATH. 1769.
EDMUND GARVEY.

Above right: *A view of Bath by Edmund Garvey where Sir William St Quintin lived towards the end of his life.*

Opposite: *Wooded Landscape with Milkmaid and Drover by Thomas Gainsborough R.A. bought by Sir William St Quintin 4th Bt.*

and the charming series of views down the River Thames by Samuel Scott reveals the influence of Willem van der Velde on his maritime painting, and the impact of Canaletto on his topography. The collection at Scampston contains just one landscape by that 'rare bird' Edmund Garvey, showing his native Bath. This was acquired in the 1760s when the elderly baronet took a house in Milsom Street in order to take the medicinal waters. It was here that he met the artist now most closely associated with him, Thomas Gainsborough.

Gainsborough and St Quentin clearly struck up a close friendship, the baronet giving the artist a horse and the artist painting the baronet's portrait (now hanging in the Entrance Hall). In the South Library cluster a trio of family half-lengths also by Gainsborough, but his finest work at Scampston is *A Wooded Landscape with a Country Wagon, Milkmaid and Drover*, which hangs in the Drawing Room. St Quintin probably bought this direct from the artist's studio after it had been exhibited in London in 1766 at the Society of Artists – he recorded in his notebook, 'Gainsborough. 1 picture. £43 11*s.* 6*d.*'. This is undoubtedly one of the artist's most attractive works from his time at Bath. It evokes the hilly countryside of the area, with beautifully controlled dappled light giving a lift and energy to the great canopy of trees. The sunlight is just allowed to peek through to illuminate the scene below. A waggoner leaning on a post is passing the time of day with a demure, pretty milkmaid. She seems unsure of his intentions and keeps her eyes downcast to avoid his gaze. The peace

of the interlude is set to be broken – the wagon horses have become restless and are setting off on their own, trundling up the incline. Only the dog has noticed and is about to bark. Whether this will allow sufficient time for the driver to catch his horses is left for the viewer to decide. It is this life and energy that sets Gainsborough's work apart from earlier British landscape artists. He is neither a topographer like Samuel Scott nor a classicist like Richard Wilson. Nor in fact are his landscapes real – he invented the settings, often working at night in his studio in Bath to create scenes from rocks, mirrors, moss and candlelight and then quickly capturing the effect by working in chalk on coloured paper. These sketches would then provide inspiration for his larger compositions. The picture at Scampston clearly shows his brilliance in creating an enchanting landscape, filled with underplayed incident and charm. It is easy to understand why Sir William chose to acquire it.

There is one last painting by Gainsborough in the house, another three-quarter length portrait that now hangs above the fireplace in the Dining Room. This shows a middle-aged man, sombre in spirit and wearing a black coat. This is the widowed William St Quintin (1729–1795). After his father's death in 1770, he owned the estate for twenty-five years and during that period transformed its landscape beyond recognition. The change was so great that when John Bigland contributed his entry to *The Beauties of England and Wales*, published in 1812, he noted that whilst the surrounding countryside was 'dull and unpicturesque', Sir William had with 'judicious taste greatly improved the scenery'. Bigland goes on to describe how 'a sterile plain destitute of every natural advantage has, at considerable expense, been rendered beautiful by art'. The genius who accomplished this was once again Lancelot 'Capability' Brown. He first came to Scampston in 1773, recording in his pocket-book: 'A journey to Scampston near Malton in Yorkshire in the autumn 17(7)3. Plans for the Bridge Building and For the Cascades . . .' This is a modest entry for such an undertaking. Brown's inclination was to create a contrived naturalistic park, with clumps of trees and, if possible, stretches of water and architectural incidents. He clearly saw these flat lands with their old-fashioned formal gardens as a great challenge. He swept away all the formal planting, opening up the space between the house and the main road as well as the views beyond. The distant hills to the east now became the natural boundary, with carefully sited trees employed to break up the view.

Brown took full advantage of the Scampston Beck, which was dammed to form three linked lakes that gently curve around the northern flank of the park. The third of these lakes passes beneath the low balustraded bridge that carries traffic towards Scarborough, allowing the road to be subtly incorporated into the scene – a true master stroke. At the head of these waters stands the Bridge Building, part folly and part bridge, with pairs of white-painted Ionic columns soaring up to support the roof with its entablature and central pediment. You can understand why Sir William commissioned Francis Nicholson, a young local artist, to paint a series of tinted drawings of Brown's grounds, including the bridge,

Opposite: *The Bridge Building as designed by Lancelot 'Capability' Brown and drawn by Francis Nicholson.*

the cascade and the Gothick tea-house in the deer park. Furthermore, he asked William Marlow (a seasoned landscape painter and a pupil of Samuel Scott) to paint views of his estate. Marlow's *View of the Lake with the Road Bridge* looks at first a little empty, with the low-lying parkland separated by the curving lake before it disappears under the bridge. Yet that is just the point – the landscape had been opened up, the distant hills fringed by trees, framing the composition. On the water sails Sir William's new sloop, bought so he could enjoy Brown's landscape from every angle.

Taking pleasure in Scampston's surroundings was certainly not confined to Sir William. The luxuriant growth of the trees has made the park even more beautiful today than when it was first conceived. Sir Charles, the current owner, says nothing gives him more enjoyment than walking in the grounds in the early evening, admiring his forebear's handiwork and foresight. A favourite moment is the approach to the bridge, with the building mirrored on the water's surface, and then he can turn to look through the columns at the lake edged by Brown's planting scheme. Charles and his wife Caroline know only too well the challenges you face when transforming a garden. In their case it was the eighteenth-century walled kitchen garden that was crying out for attention. For years this had been in a sad state, with commercial Christmas trees supplanting regimented rows of vegetables, and with its outbuildings and greenhouses on their last legs. Instead of accepting the inevitable, or trying to turn the clock back, they chose to follow in the Scampston tradition and took the decision to create something entirely novel.

Walking west from the house you first encounter the eighteenth-century brick stable block, the cart shed and then a long brick wall. Here Caroline directed me towards a small wooden door that gives no hint of the surprise on the other side – the sheer scale of their enterprise. The walled garden is a giant, stretching for four and a half acres, and it has been transformed in its entirety. Inside the walls are long walks bordered by beds, with trees and hedges that occasionally open to afford you enchanting views across the great space. Initially you might expect these views to be similar but every one is different, ranging from the tranquil Green Garden with mown lawns, pool and yew columns standing like sentinels, to the Serpentine Garden with its weaving waves of yews – the tops left to grow out naturally to let them sway in the breeze. The garden defies all your expectations. At the centre is the Meadow Garden, with a riot of colourful perennials set amongst grasses, and here a splashing fountain provides noise and life, taking up the vigour of the flowers and complementing the delicate movement of the grasses.

The complexity of the design and the brilliant orchestration of the shapes and colours can be seen best from a high grass mound at the upper end. Here your view expands to take in the interlocking spaces, some abutting and others divided by green corridors. The contemporary genius behind it all is Piet Oudolf. His work was known to Charles and Caroline, yet she recalls how stunned she was when she first saw his designs – she knew instantly that he had got it exactly right. His talent lies in two distinct areas: first, the ability to see gardens in three dimensions and second, an enviable knowledge of plants from their earliest growth through to their decrepitude. He makes use of the plants in all their stages, incorporating buds, flowers and seed heads in his plans. These talents mean that his gardens are skilfully designed to look good throughout the year. On a bright summer's day your eye may be caught by contrasting colours set against the sharp shadows of the hedges whilst in the depth of winter it would be the sight of frozen seed heads threaded together with glistening spiders' webs, seen in silhouette against a brick wall. This garden is all the more remarkable when you learn that the vast majority of plants were propagated here – Caroline estimates in one case 6,500 were grown from fifty original *Molinas Caerulea* plants. The same energy and flair that created the first of the formal gardens with its axial canal, and which went into widening the Scampston Beck to create the series of lakes, has now been devoted to this more confined space. It comes as no surprise to learn that it is already considered to be one of the best contemporary gardens in Britain.

With the death of the 5th Baronet in 1795, the estate passed to his nephew, William Thomas Darby, who took the additional surname of St Quintin. This young man looks rather serious in his portrait by John Opie, perhaps because of the spectacles he wears, yet serious or not he was clearly delighted by his good fortune. At the age of 26 he came north from his native Hampshire to discover a house, modified only slightly since it was built in the seventeenth century, sitting in a spanking new park. This in itself may well have provided sufficient motivation for him to embark on a project to remodel the house. There was also the question of practical necessity. Since the 1730s Scampston had been largely a bachelor's dwelling – certainly no children were raised there. Yet in the first decade of his ownership William and his wife, Arabella Calcroft, had no fewer than ten children! The first the world knew of the changes came with the appearance at the Royal Academy in 1803 of *A View of Scampston House, Yorkshire: now building for W. T. St. Quintin, Esq.* by Thomas Leverton. Both the architect and his patron must have been pleased with their design, and with every justification. It worked brilliantly, both outside and in.

Externally Leverton retained the outer walls on the south façade but reduced the projecting sides and lowered the hipped roof, covering the façade with stucco. He made the central bay the chief feature, creating a large semi-circle or bow, articulated with austere pilasters that matched the only other decoration on this elevation, the equally severe architraves above the ground-floor windows. The bow rises up through the roofline, ringed by the balustrade, and there soars into a great dome – a highly unusual feature in English domestic architecture. It was and is a brilliant *tour de force*, giving a dynamism to the whole elevation. A similar treatment was used on the west front, where Leverton created the new entrance. The walls are again given a minimum of decorative detail but at the centre stands an even more dramatic bow. The pilasters here are replaced by columns that rise to carry the semi-circular shape through to the balustrade. The centre is taken by a pair of double doors, articulated with matching rectangular, circular and square panels. The whole is very smart and, again, very understated.

Entering the semi-circular Hall, you discover that Leverton has used this double-door motif everywhere to articulate his interiors, although inside they are made of rich mahogany with vertical panels interrupted by large circles – a discreet reflection of the design of his façades. To the left you pass into the Morning Room,

and to the right the Drawing Room. Here Leverton reveals his next surprise. On the south side behind the principal façade he has created an enfilade of reception rooms, each in the most fashionable style of the day. The Drawing Room is followed by a Library and then Dining Room, all laid out as a Regency man of taste would wish: decorum and moderation being the order. Each room has large south-facing windows that stretch down to the floor, affording wonderful views across the park. The Drawing Room is plainly decorated, save for a rich cornice and a white marble fireplace in the centre. The Dining Room is articulated in a similar style and features a columned recess for a sideboard (then the latest piece of furniture).

It is, however, the Library where Leverton's decoration is seen at its most brilliant. The walls are given an extraordinary delicacy, with a gilded plaster frieze along the upper edge that alternates vases and leaves, held in place by pilasters painted to look like marble. Between these are the bookcases, built into the walls and headed with more half-circles. At the far end is the bow, contained within by a pair of columns, and at the other the fireplace flanked by bookcases. Leverton's delight in balance means that here he has to play a trick: the bookcase to the left is a fake – a disguised door that leads into a further library beyond.

Leverton's new library was simply not large enough to contain the great collection of books acquired by the St Quintins over the previous fifty years. These books, like so much else at Scampston, reveal the owners' enquiring minds. Philosophy, religion and literature are all well represented, as indeed are science and travel. Deep in the lower shelves are the 5th Baronet's copies of *Captain Cook's Voyage to the South Pacific*, acquired as they were published in the late 1770s. Here Sir William could follow the exploits of his Yorkshire contemporary as he met with the natives of New Zealand and mapped unexplored coastlines. The second library also reveals how Leverton had to work within the constraints of his patron's pocket. It is clear that St Quintin did not have sufficient funds to allow for an entirely new house, so behind the principal rooms, adaptation was the order of the day. This much earlier room was modified to contain a further range of neoclassical bookcases. Beyond it, the late-seventeenth-century staircase was retained for secondary use, but Leverton cleverly managed to fit a new

Opposite: *Leverton's enfilade looking from the South Library through the double doors into the Drawing Room.*

Above: *A French commode attributed to Francois Oeben that has decended to Scampston from the Mills Collection inlaid with amaranth and kingwood.*

main staircase between the north library and his Entrance Hall. The single rise bifurcates on a half landing beneath a large circular window that floods the small space with light. The banisters are designed in a simple trellis pattern, so as not to distract. You cannot help but smile at Leverton's ingenuity.

The portraits of Sir Charles Legard's antecedents now hang in the Staircase Hall. The family have been in Yorkshire as long as the St Quintins, and were also given a baronetcy in the seventeenth century. In 1754 Sir Digby Legard, 5th Bt. (c.1730–1773), went on his Grand Tour and whilst in Rome he sat for that most fashionable portraitist, Pompeo Batoni. The elegant result now hangs near the portrait of the young lady he married the following year, Miss Jane Cartwright. She is shown well dressed and wreathed in pearls, not only on her dress but also adorning her hair. It is a fine and characteristic performance by the equally young Joseph Wright, who hailed from Derby but who spent his summers journeying around the towns of the north Midlands, picking up commissions such as this. Both these paintings were brought to Scampston by Sir Charles's father, having

previously hung at the family seat at nearby Ganton. The large white marble statue of the Venus Marina had a longer journey – although not from Rome as the name might suggest, but from Roehampton in Middlesex. In 1802 Lord Bessborough's collection at Manresa House had to be sold. Among the statuary was this Venus Marina, sculpted for the earl by Joseph Wilton. The young owner of Scampston obviously considered it was just the piece he needed for the house he was about to remodel and paid over £100 to secure it. She now stands in the Entrance Hall, the naked goddess turning into the room with her hands protecting her modesty. This pose serves a secondary purpose, allowing Wilton to displace the weight of her right arm by connecting the tips of her fingers to her breast with small pegs. At her feet a lively dolphin disports itself on a 'beach' of roughened marble carved with the semblance of waves. Sadly the young connoisseur William St Quintin did not live long enough to enjoy fully either his works of art or his house. He died unexpectedly in January 1805, aged only 35, leaving a widow and nine surviving children.

As is often the case after a period of rebuilding, his death was followed by a period of repose. What is more unusual at Scampston is that the period should have lasted until relatively recently. The reason, often a shortage of funds, was certainly initially the case here, but compounded by the mental instability of his heir, another William, and thereafter the succession of the estate to his brother, Matthew, who by then was aged 59. He and his wife seem to have made few changes beyond wallpapering the Drawing Room; it is somehow typical that this too has survived until today. Indeed, until the present owners' arrival the only significant change in the appearance of the house since the early nineteenth century had been the arrival of works of art inherited from the collector and highly successful London banker Sir Charles Mills, 1st Bt. (1792–1872). Mills had a penchant for French eighteenth-century art and would regularly break his journey back from the city to buy porcelain and furniture. At Scampston are a number of particularly good pieces of Sèvres that he acquired, including a rare pair of candlesticks with twisted Solomonic columns and delicate trays, all in a mixture of colours (including one Caroline calls 'horrid pink'). From the Mills collection also came a very handsome French commode inlaid with amaranth and kingwood, made in Paris in the mid 1750s. This shows a simplicity of design, especially when compared with the writhing rococo forms popular a few years earlier. Its design suggests that it may well have been made by François Oeben, the leading *eboniste* of the day who was patronized by Louis XV and his mistress, Madame de Pompadour. A number of similar commodes were supplied to their apartments at Versailles.

This commode now sits in the Drawing Room, where Caroline has effected a skilful transformation. When she and Charles came to the house in the mid 1990s the room was shut up, seldom used. Large and ungainly pieces of furniture had found their way there and early family portraits hung rather incongruously against the florid mid-nineteenth-century wallpaper. The Legards were determined that this room should play its rightful part in the enfilade and tackled its restoration with care and gusto. Caroline, who had worked for the National Trust, knew just whom to call on for assistance, and friends and former colleagues came and helped. The wallpaper was cleaned with India rubbers and the brass rails that criss-cross the bookcases in the Library were sent to London for dip-cleaning. Here and elsewhere paint scrapings were carried out, allowing the rooms to be returned either to their original decorative schemes or an improved version. Paintings were taken down, furniture was put into store and the rooms gradually emptied of their surplus contents. It must almost have seemed as if Leverton had returned!

The house was always full of noise, hustle and bustle and with a heady sense of excitement as the years of neglect were put right. Now only photographs bring back memories of the previous state, as the restoration is so complete and such a success that all traces of neglect have been banished. Scampston has been returned to more than its former glory, and the same is now true of the walled garden. Finally, it seems that all the efforts focused historically on either house or landscape have come together. The hard work and ingenuity of generations of the family since the arrival of St Quentin in the early eighteenth century has now paid off in full. From the road the house stands proud, displaying a confidence that will surely see it through another century, as it passes from the hands of Charles and Caroline to those of the next generation, his son Christopher and wife Miranda.

Opposite: *The Venus Marina formerly owned by the Earl of Bessborough and acquired by William Darby St Quintin in 1801 standing in the entrance hall.*

Above: *Pair of Sèvres Solomonic candlesticks decorated with flowers from the Mills collection.*

Sherborne Castle, Dorset

The seat of the Wingfield-Digby Family

It is really only from the rooftops – four storeys and many stairs up – that you begin to appreciate the perfect setting of this castle. Sherborne stands in a valley, surrounded by clean-shaven hills, delicately planted with a fringe of trees. Running from east to west down the middle of the valley run the old main road, the later railway and the ancient watercourse. The River Yeo rises just to the east, in the hills above Milborne Port, and as it descends into the Sherborne valley it forms a series of lakes beneath the castle before it flows on towards Yeovil. Shifting your gaze to the north you see the hills that rise above Poynington and Sandford Orcas which form a natural boundary. Nearer, and to the west, is the town of Sherborne itself with its magnificent medieval abbey and, in the foreground, the ruins of a great castle that date from the same era. Finally, looking to the south, the hills again rise up to Goathill, Haydon, and North Wootton.

This is ancient Wessex, old England. Formerly at the very heart of civil and ecclesiastical government, it has slipped into an honourable retirement since the late Middle Ages. This is a landscape flecked with medieval villages bearing ancient-sounding names, all now remarkably peaceful. Yet the scale of the abbey and old castle in Sherborne tell of the earlier period when the town was more important than Salisbury, and its bishop required the protection of a castle. Whilst Sherborne Castle was originally conceived as part of that ecclesiastical medieval domain, it has since been transformed from a hunting lodge into a great country house. The castle is a delicious hybrid, a mixture of what was first intended and what it actually became. Its unusual form and the beauty of its surroundings have delighted successive generations of owners. From Sir Walter Raleigh to the Earls of Bristol and their kinsmen the Digbys. It has now descended to John and Jo Wingfield-Digby, who share its pleasures with their son and his wife, Edward and Maria.

Life was never quite so settled for the first owner, Sir Walter Raleigh (1554–1618). He was granted the lease on the ancient castle and its estates in 1591, a reward for his achievements at the court of Elizabeth I. His had been a meteoric rise. By the early sixteenth century the Raleighs were a well-established Devon family, albeit one of no great consequence. Raleigh was born in 1554 and saw action with the Huguenot armies in France in the late 1560s before going up to Oriel College, Oxford. From there, like many before and since, he sought to establish his position by studying the law, and was admitted to the Middle Temple in London in 1575. His straitened financial circumstances were recorded by the seventeenth-century pedagogue John Aubrey in his book *Brief Lives*, where he noted that Thomas Child, a contemporary of Raleigh's at Oxford, said that Walter was so short of money that he had to 'borrow a gown of him . . . which he never returned, nor money for it'.

Drawn towards the court in the late 1570s, Raleigh responded to every opportunity that came his way. On one occasion he served as a naval captain on the *Falcon* as part of his cousin Humphrey Gilbert's exploratory force 'to remote, heathen and barbarous lands'. On another he served as a soldier in Ireland to repress the Earl of Desmond's rebellion. By 1581, the 27-year-old Raleigh had caught the queen's eye. He was physically striking, very tall for the period with a pale, refined face framed by a mass of dark hair. He could turn an elegant poem and charm his monarch with sudden audacious courtesy, famously spreading his cloak over 'this plashy place'. His rise was rapid. He was knighted in 1585, made Lord Lieutenant of Cornwall, Vice-Admiral of the West, and succeeded Sir Christopher Hatton as Captain of the Guards. By 1591, when he came to Sherborne, he had already been granted Durham Place, between the Strand and the Thames, for his London house, lands in Derbyshire and a vast estate of 42,000 acres in Ireland. He was like a brilliant, energetic butterfly, one minute composing intricate verses praising his sovereign, the next devising expeditions to the New World (where he colonized Virginia, named in her honour). His name is linked with exciting innovations, from the growing of potatoes (which he may have first introduced to his lands in Ireland) to the use of tobacco. (Whilst he cannot truly be credited with its actual import, he was probably the courtier who made smoking it such a fashionable pursuit.) At his apogee he was the very model of the Elizabethan courtier – cultivated, brave, energetic and handsome, and unattached to any but his queen.

In 1589 Bishop Piers of Salisbury died. The bishopric's extensive estate included the old castle at Sherborne that had been built by Bishop Rose of Salisbury between 1107 and 1135. It had been well maintained, and as the contemporary historian John Leyland notes, 'there be few peaces of work yn England of antiquity of this that standith so whole and so well couchid'. Raleigh would have seen Sherborne many times on his frequent journeys along the old main road between London and his native Devon. He clearly coveted it, and started to petition for the estate immediately following the bishop's demise. A less

impetuous queen acceded and it was his, on a ninety-nine-year lease for the sum of £390 per annum. (Elizabeth could strike a hard bargain, even with her favourites!) Raleigh had attained a country estate to compare with his fellow courtiers. His initial intention seems to have been to remodel the old castle as a suitably grand establishment, but no sooner had he received Sherborne than matters at court went awry. A clandestine marriage to the queen's maid of honour, Elizabeth Throckmorton (which had been kept secret despite her giving birth to their son) was revealed and Raleigh and his wife were dispatched by the queen to the Tower of London. On their release at the end of 1592, the couple were banished to Sherborne.

Whilst Raleigh set to rebuilding the old castle, he also turned his attention to the bishop's Hunting Lodge, set on steeply rising ground to the south, where he probably intended to live during the building work at the old castle itself. With advice from Adrian Gilbert, his half-brother, he commenced work on the Lodge almost immediately and by 1594 the first stage was complete. His building consisted of a compact tower with kitchens in the basement, a central hall and large parlour on the ground floor, with a similar arrangement of rooms on the floors above. These remain the core of the present building.

By 1599 the queen had not only relented and reinstated Raleigh fully at court, but had also converted the lease of Sherborne into an outright gift. On hearing this good news, Raleigh made plans to carry out yet more building work. Some of these designs survive in the Cecil Archive in Hatfield. One reveals the next stage, with four new hexagonal towers rising at each corner; one to contain a staircase, the others purely ornamental, creating a series of delightful 'look-out rooms'. Raleigh himself seems to have had a study at the very top, and the final flight of stairs leading to it (now reached through later attics) shows the sophistication of his work. The design of the banisters has been carefully considered: slender swelling columns with bases and small capitals supported by large newel posts of the same form. Elsewhere, elaborate plasterwork ceilings adorned the principal rooms and heraldic stone beasts, including Raleigh's crest the roebuck, enlivened the roofline. According to John Coker's *Survey of Dorset*, 'in the park adjoining . . . he beautified with orchards, gardens and groves, of much variety and delight, that whether you consider the goodness of the soil, the pleasantness of the seat, and other delicacies belonging to it, it [Sherborne] is unparalleled by any in these parts'.

The intricacies of Raleigh's gardens, with their highly artificial approach to nature, are another aspect of that love of artifice and ornament characteristic of late-sixteenth-century England. This is also revealed in the magnificent painting hanging in the Red Drawing Room depicting an imaginary royal progress. Queen Elizabeth, held aloft by her courtiers, moves through the streets of London watched by her subjects. Yet the image is not so straightforward – artifice lurks everywhere. Firstly, in the depiction of the queen – this is no aging matriarch, a monarch who has sat on her throne longer than any of her Tudor predecessors; instead she is young, slender, with masses of hair and wearing a dress almost overloaded with jewels. This is just how she had decreed it. Turning then to the courtiers – are they really carrying her? No, merely holding aloft a light canopy, supported on four poles – a canopy almost as decorated as the queen's dress, with its artful arrangement of stitched flowers topped by ostrich feathers. The hard work is being done by the Yeomen of the Guard behind, who are pushing a wheeled trolley supporting the queen's throne. And the houses are equally false, being derived from contemporary architectural treaties rather that a true representation of the timber-fronted buildings that lined the streets of her capital.

By the end of Elizabeth's reign Raleigh had completed work on the lodge, creating a highly distinctive building adjacent to the old castle where work was still proceeding. He would surely have expected this to have passed in due course to his son and heir, Walter. However this was not to be. After the queen's death in

1603 Raleigh's world began to crumble. He did not find favour with James I and the king's minister, Robert Cecil, seems to have so arranged matters that Raleigh was implicated in the treasonous Main Plot. Raleigh was dispatched once again to the Tower. At Sherborne there are two legal documents that explain his eventual loss of the estate. As Edward Wingfield-Digby explains, in the first of these, Raleigh puts it into trust for his son, distancing it from himself, hoping to avoid its potential seizure by the Crown. The second is the Crown's response. James I's advisors, having studied the first document, pronounced it invalid. Raleigh was then forced to sign away his estates. His signature at its close is tiny, elaborately formed. You can feel the heartache of this disillusioned prisoner who would go to his death on Tower Hill in 1618.

Following their confiscation by the Crown, the Sherborne estates followed a chequered path for the next decade, oscillating between James I and his eldest son, Prince Henry, and the royal favourite Robert Carr, Earl of Somerset. The latter's career waned, and following his attainder in 1617 Sherborne was sold by the king at a discounted price to a bright diplomatic star, John Digby (1580–1653). Digby was a younger son who had climbed the ladder of success through the law and thereafter at court. He became the English ambassador to Spain, and was rich enough to pay £10,000 for the Sherborne lands. But thereafter his career see-sawed, and much of the 1620s and 30s were spent away from court living at Sherborne. Like Raleigh, he favoured the new Lodge over the old castle, enlarging it by building four symmetrical two-storeyed wings running from Raleigh's turrets out to turrets of his own. The top of his building was enlivened with further sculpture and the new large courtyard decorated with elaborate stonework. Inside, the rooms were given even more intricate plaster ceilings and provided with gigantic fireplaces. The decorative details, almost to the point of exhaustion, were based on his coat of arms as Earl of Bristol, the title bestowed on him by James I in 1622.

The Red Drawing Room on the ground floor is the supreme surviving interior of this period. The ceiling is a rich mixture of ornamental ribs, each containing heraldic beasts and flowers, whilst the double-height fireplace still survives, with its classical fluted Corinthian columns flanking the grate in the lower half and a colossal coat of arms in the upper panel. The fireplace in the Green Drawing Room is even bigger, with double Corinthian columns, and here the coat of arms is caught up in a confection of exaggerated strapwork decoration, entwined by monstrous heads. This is celebratory decoration on a grand scale, reflecting Sherborne's new owner, who was confident enough of his abilities and his newly acquired status to take on both the Duke of Buckingham and the young Charles I when necessary.

Not all his work is so powerfully demonstrative, however. There is a lightness of touch in the carved woodwork above the highly unusual entrances to the Oak Hall. Here the coat of arms and the family's device of the *fleur-de-lys* are

cut out like silhouettes, whilst the heraldic beasts, carved in the round, act as guards in the four corners. At either side of the hall Lord Bristol created small double-doored kiosks. Rather like the screens used in medieval times, these were designed to prevent heat from escaping the room. No other entrances of this type appear to have survived, and it may be that the Sherborne pair are unique.

Walking around the house with John Wingfield-Digby, you become very aware of his ancestors. The walls are covered with their portraits and those of families connected to them through marriage. Whilst no paintings at Sherborne depict the 1st Lord Bristol, the next generation can be seen in portraits by Sir Anthony van Dyck. The grandest composition, now hanging on the end wall of the Green Drawing Room, is the splendid double portrait of Lord Bristol's eldest son John,

Opposite: *The Green Drawing Room, formerly Sir Walter Raleigh's Great Chamber, and with a plaster ceiling bearing his coat of arms. The fireplace is the most flamboyant of those created for the 1st Earl of Bristol. The wallpaper was designed by Owen Jones circa 1860.*

Left: *One of the curious two-door porches in the Oak Room devised for the 1st Earl of Bristol and topped with decorative elements derived from his coat of arms.*

Lord Digby (1612–1677), and his brother-in-law, William Russell, Earl of Bedford (1616–1700). The prime version of this is now in the Spencer Collection at Althorp, Northamptonshire. That at Sherborne was probably painted towards the end of the seventeenth century as a fitting memorial to the family's position at the court of Charles I. Van Dyck not only captures Digby's cherubic good looks, haloed by a cascade of fair hair, but also his arrogance. You can readily believe that by the time this was painted Digby had had to cool his heels in the Fleet Prison, having fought a duel with William Croft in the precincts of the court at Whitehall (a fight he naturally won). In this portrait he and his brother-in-law appear the epitome of young cavaliers. It is a surprise to discover that both were critics of Charles I and kept aloof from court. Unfortunately for the king, Digby later changed his allegiances. His policies and his often overbearing attitude to the monarch's other supporters were partly responsible for the king's defeat and eventual execution.

Downstairs in the Red Drawing Room there are further versions of portraits by Van Dyck. Three of them chart one of the saddest love stories of the early seventeenth century, that of Sir Kenelm Digby (1602–1665) and his wife, Venetia. Kenelm, a distant cousin of Lord Bristol, was brought up in pious seclusion

Above: *Portrait of Kenelm Digby, his wife Venetia and their two children after Sir Anthony Van Dyck.*

Opposite: *Venetia Digby on her deathbed. A miniature based on a painting by Sir Anthony Van Dyck.*

at Gayhurst in Northamptonshire, following his father's execution for his role in the Gunpowder Plot. His childhood sweetheart, Venetia Stanley, who lived nearby, was frowned on as a potential match. Yet, after forced separation, travel and a good deal of misunderstanding, they secretly married in 1624. The first of these portraits, dated 1632, depicts a jovial Sir Kenelm, happy and contented with his beautiful wife and two young sons, Kenelm and John. After years of frustration and deception, all seems serene. Sadly this happiness was shattered a year later, when Venetia died in her bed whilst an unaware Sir Kenelm was entertaining a friend in his parlour. It seems likely that she succumbed to arsenic poisoning, caused by the face powder she wore to keep her complexion pale. Whatever its cause, Sir Kenelm viewed her death as an act of divine punishment for his sins. He wrote to his brother that his 'torment must never have an end whilst I live . . . I can have no physician but death'. He commemorated Venetia's passing by ordering a death mask and also commissioned Van Dyck to paint her posthumously, her head resting on a pillow. The final of these portraits is of Sir Kenelm alone. Gone are the blowsy high spirits of his youth: now the bright clothes have been replaced with the black of mourning, his hair is worn long and a beard is growing, melancholy has overtaken his bright air; and all this in the space of two years.

A few years later the Carolean life was was swept away by the Civil War, a process mirrored at Sherborne. The old fortified castle was a repeated target for Parliamentary forces, controlling as it did the principal road from London to the west. Lord Bristol and his son were often absent on royal business but a letter from the Earl of Bedford seems to have secured the safety of Sherborne for both Lady Bristol and her daughter-in-law, Bedford's own sister. The castle was left unharmed but the old castle finally succumbed to General Fairfax's troops in 1645, and was subsequently largely demolished. Both Bristol and his son, Lord Digby, took refuge on the continent, the former dying there in 1653. After the Restoration, Lord Digby, now 2nd Earl of Bristol, returned, but again he was out of kilter with his age. His espousal of the Catholic faith prevented him from holding any official post. He died at his house in Chelsea in 1677.

He (or perhaps his son) is likely to have remodelled the wings to the east front of the new castle with fine classical windows applied to the Jacobean façade. Originally with casements, and now with large plate glass, they are almost startling in their newness. In the space of a century the castle's architecture had developed rapidly, from a fantasy of turrets and towers to a reflection of classical Italian buildings. Lord Bristol clearly wanted to stay abreast of architectural fashion, especially as the old castle had been totally given up and the former lodge, Sherborne Castle, was now the permanent seat of the Earls of Bristol.

However, it is at exactly this point that the main line failed and the Bristol title became extinct. John Digby, the only son of the 2nd Earl, inherited in 1677 but left no heir twenty years later. Thus the Sherborne estates passed to his distant cousin, William Digby, Lord Digby of Geashill (1662–1752). His, the elder branch of the Digby family, had long lived at Coleshill in Warwickshire, but he quickly recognized that Sherborne offered a larger and more attractive estate and moved there with his wife, Lady Jane Noel, and their brood of children. Here he carefully managed the estate for more than fifty years, living to the age of 90. Upon his death in 1752, his eldest son having predeceased him, the whole estate was left to his grandson Edward, then a young man of 22. His was a sensational inheritance: the land and the castle, some £23,000 in the bank and an additional £14,000 to clear any debts and for the care of William Digby's other grandchildren. Edward, together with his mother and his four younger brothers, moved into the castle later in the year. Naturally he initiated some projects to celebrate his inheritance, the first being the remodelling of the park. Up to that point, the castle had been surrounded by formal gardens, much admired by Alexander Pope in the 1720s, with an ancient deer park beyond. This was all transformed through the genius of 'Capability' Brown. It was Brown's first project in the West Country, and he recognized that it could usefully enhance his reputation.

In 1753 he drew up plans to dam the River Yeo and create a series of serpentine lakes, gently dropping down the valley from below Crackmore in the east and passing beneath the castle before the water rejoined the old river course outside the town. This would separate the new castle from the ruins of the old and gave Brown the opportunity to turn those into a Gothick folly, with the addition of a new crenellated wall and a bastion wreathed in ivy. Here and elsewhere new trees were introduced, some to act as screens, others to create points of interest, and overall to provide a gentle green curtain around the edge of the park.

A similar buzz of activity pervaded the house. Even the dry estate accounts reflect the youthful energy of Edward and his family. We can see how rooms were decorated, chimneys swept, furniture and clocks repaired. A Mr Hoddinott of Sherborne supplied new textiles, and Mr Thackwaite of London new tables and chairs. Paintings and books were sent down from Coleshill. The former were hung around the house but the latter posed more of a problem. But this acted as a catalyst for young Digby's most audacious innovation – his new Library. Formed out of the ground floor of the south-east wing, nothing in the rest of the building prepares you for the surprise of this most cosmopolitan room. Walking to it through richly panelled and painted rooms, its design, and indeed its colour (or rather, the lack of it), come as a shock. It is a spectacular piece of Gothick revival decoration, a reflection of the buildings erected by those sophisticated and cultivated connoisseurs who surrounded Horace Walpole, the arbiter of contemporary taste. Often termed 'Strawberry Hill Gothick' after Walpole's house by the Thames, the style allows for the most playful interpretations of motifs derived from medieval buildings. At Sherborne, Frances Cartwright of Bryanston devised the plaster ceiling with its tracery and trailing flowers, whilst the bookcases, replete with ogee heads interspersed with circular niches, are the work of Mr Ride. The room is painted a flat white throughout, warmth being provided by the richness of the wide oak floorboards and from graduated shelves of leather-bound books, together with the portrait of Sir Kenelm Digby over the fine white marble fireplace.

The Gothick delicacy exhibited here is also to be found in a delightful dairy, commissioned by Edward Digby at around the same time, probably for his mother, Lady Charlotte. The present chatelaine, Jo Wingfield-Digby, who has already done so much to improve the gardens, is equally delighted by the room. Lying just beneath the castle, between the courtyard and the grass terrace, you enter the single chamber through a tripartite Gothick screen topped with pinnacles and crenellations. Inside, the colour is as cool and refined as the Library. A simple Gothick frieze gives life to the ceiling whilst the walls are protected by off-white tiles. Here the ladies of the house would separate curds from whey and make thick cream, butter, cheese and such eighteenth-century delights as junket and syllabub. It is a small folly with a practical purpose – just the sort of building that might be thrown up by a cultivated young man who had inherited a fortune.

The unexpected death of Edward in 1757, only five years after he came into the estate, did not interrupt the remarkable flow of improvements. The baton simply passed to his brother, Henry Digby (1731–1793), 7th Lord Digby. He obviously shared his elder brother's taste, completing the Gothick Library and commissioning further improvements to the grounds from 'Capability' Brown. He even had his portrait painted by John Giles Eccardt, an artist much favoured by Walpole and his circle. This is an elegant reminder of times past – the young Henry is shown in Van Dyck dress, a reflection of the portraits of his seventeenth-century ancestors.

The new Lord Digby also developed a taste and style of his own – more lavish and more diverse. During the 1760s the house was again alive with builders and joiners; old windows, dados and doors were replaced. For the remodelled rooms, furniture was commissioned from the smartest London outlets, with the lion's share going to the great partnership of Mayhew & Ince. Their 'catalogue', *Universal Systems of Household Furniture*, was published in 1762 and we can assume Henry Digby received a copy that year. It remains in the Library at Sherborne today. Its original plates offered enticing alternative ideas for complete rooms and ornamental decoration as well as a wealth of different pieces of furniture. As tempting now as it was then, it certainly caught Henry's imagination. By the time he came to settle Mayhew & Ince's final invoice in 1785, he had spent an amazing total of £2,190 0s. 0d.

Henry's bank account for 1762 also reveals a payment to the outstanding Anglo-French cabinetmaker, Pierre Langlois, with another bill was submitted two years later. Langlois is likely to be the maker of the two magnificent pier tables and looking glasses that stand between the windows in the Red Drawing Room. The simple idea of having mirrors between the windows to reflect the gentle light of candles placed on the supporting tables is taken here to an extreme form. The table tops are supported by the figures of ostriches, their animated forms giving them a lively, even cross, countenance. The ostriches, carved in wood, coated in gesso and finally covered in gold leaf, are evocative of the supporters on the Digby coat of arms. The mahogany tops of the tables are stunningly inlaid with a variety of coloured woods, giving the impression of a scattering of flowers. The looking glasses themselves are carved with figures of two monkeys at the tops, holding aloft the Digby *fleur-de-lys* in a cartouche with their baron's coronet above. On either side a pair of architectural herms is seen in profile, supporting lattice baskets of flowers, and further flowers are carved as if tumbling from their scroll supports. Across the mirrored surfaces are ribbons and festoons, all of gilded wood. This is not a purely decorative device. The London makers had not yet devised a method to make large single sheets of mirrored glass, so these pieces of wood obscured numerous joins. The ingenuity of the design and the sheer brilliance of Langlois's work is breathtaking – as is the lavishness of Lord Digby's patronage.

Opposite: *The Gothick Dairy created for Lady Charlotte Digby circa 1760.*

Whilst the pier tables are a full response to the prevailing rich late-rococo style of the 1760s, the Orangery, commissioned by Lord Digby nearly twenty years later, shows him turning to the new Francophile classicism associated with its creator, Henry Holland (son-in-law of 'Capability' Brown). This elegant building has all the studied discipline one expects to find in the work of the architect who would go on to create Carlton House in Pall Mall for the Prince of Wales, and who remodelled the interiors of Woburn, Althorp and Southill. The pair of pedimented porticos, sparse use of pilasters and repeated Coade stone decoration in the frieze are typical of Holland. At this early point in his career, though, his patron felt at ease in proposing modifications to his architect's ideas. Holland had originally designed the room to include an additional door at the middle; Lord Digby, now mature and confident in his tastes, had other ideas, noting on the plan 'no door here but the window to be the same height as the others'.

Just when you feel all this building work must have been reaching a conclusion, you discover that a new project had been taken up. In the late 1780s Evan Owan commenced work on a new wing to house the kitchen, further bedrooms and the servants' quarters. In July 1787 Lord Digby wrote that 'we came here the first of the month and found our house full of workmen and some rubbish. In about a month's time we hope to get our kitchen finished'. (Some things never change!) The kitchen was finally completed and supplied with smart new copper pots and pans, all inscribed with his initials and some with their capacities. These are now found arranged in the basement kitchen of Raleigh's original house – the lids still fit as tightly as ever.

It is fortunate that all this refurbishment was completed by the late summer of 1787 as George III and his family, who were staying close by at Weymouth, came to visit during August. Bands played, deputations delivered speeches, meals were cooked and served and a justifiably proud Lord and Lady Digby took their royal guests on a tour of the building. It must have struck a chord with the king, whose own work at Windsor reflected a similar balance between honouring the past and delighting in modern comforts. The smart new furniture included an ingenious dressing table with a fold-out top, ratcheted mirror and a myriad useful compartments, just the thing Queen Charlotte would find useful when attending to her hair after a carriage ride in the park. One wonders if the royal visitors also saw the suite of painted furniture that now stands in the Blue Drawing Room, beneath Gainsborough's splendid portrait of their host. One of

the tables has a very distinctive top made from polished ammonites, fossils found embedded in the South Dorset cliffs. The visit was such a success that George III made his host Lord Digby an Earl – a dignity he held for just six years, before he died in 1793.

History then partly repeated itself, as the early nineteenth century saw a prolonged period of inactivity and careful replenishing of the family fortune under his son and heir, Edward, 2nd Earl Digby (1773–1856). There was neither wife nor children to spur him on, and thus Sherborne escaped any picturesque Regency or early-Victorian modification, a fate which befell many other early houses. Edward's only close relation was his sister, Lady Charlotte Digby. In 1796 she had married a successful lawyer and Member of Parliament, William Wingfield Baker (1775–1858), and it was to their son George Digby Wingfield (1797–1883) that Edward left his estate, together with a carefully nurtured fortune reported to stand at £1 million.

Inactivity creates its own problems as well as its rewards. The castle was in a sorry state when George inherited it, but he was swift to put this right. Despite being in his sixties, George (who took the additional surname of Digby by royal licence) embarked on a programme of restoration. In the first instance, the architect Philip Hardwicke was commissioned to restore, rather than rebuild, the castle; a task he carried out admirably. The changes made by preceding owners were retained rather than swept away. Seventeenth-century ceilings were repaired, the eighteenth-century Gothick library was repainted and the external stonework refaced. The only room that George had remodelled was Raleigh's parlour on the ground floor. Today this is aptly presided over by Sir Francis Grant's great portrait of George Wingfield-Digby astride his hunter. Even here the work reflects his respect for the past style of the castle: the panelling, ribbed

Opposite: The Blue Drawing Room with the portrait of the 1st Earl Digby by Thomas Gainsborough R.A. to the right of the mirror.

Above left: A painted side table circa 1780 standing in the Blue Drawing Room with cut ammonites laid into its top.

Above right: Detail of the 'GDWD' monogram on the Solarium fireplace.

Opposite: The Solarium, originally Sir Walter Raleigh's Great Parlour, remodelled by George Wingfield-Digby circa 1760, with a colossal fireplace executed by White & Co. The full-length portraits, both by Sir Francis Grant, depict Anne Eliza Murray Stewart, née Wingfield-Digby and George Wingfield-Digby mounted on his hunter.

ceilings, windows and even a fireplace derived from elsewhere. This fireplace is every bit as exuberant as those designed for Lord Bristol 250 years earlier. But Victorians could summon up even more sumptuous building materials and the contractors, White & Co., did not disappoint. George Digby Wingfield-Digby's coat of arms is flanked by richly veined marble, carved with a medley of his initials, GDWD, intricately interwoven. This room, and the Green Drawing Room above, are furnished with contemporary English furniture supplied by Morants & Holland, often in the French style. The curtains and wallpaper, designed by Owen Jones and supplied by Warners, have miraculously survived, although the turquoise-based wallpaper is just a little faded and the similarly patterned curtains are starting to fray. These deficiencies are soon to be remedied by the present owners as part of the ongoing process of gentle refurbishment they are undertaking with a sensitivity that would have appealed to their ancestors. All aspects of this house and its gardens are coming to life once again under the care and watchful eyes of John and Jo Wingfield-Digby.

Looking after Sherborne involves striking a balance between the commercial necessities of the twenty-first century and the preservation of part of England that has been nurtured by John's family for nearly 400 years. That is not to say that the pioneering qualities of John, Lord Bristol, and Edward and Henry Digby have vanished – far from it. John Wingfield-Digby has added innovations of his own, including a vineyard on the estate which produces a range of first-rate wines. In early autumn the grapes hang lusciously down, ripe for picking, save those that are harvested early by John's labrador! It is somewhat appropriate that the family's good fortune can now be toasted with their own champagne; a good fortune that looks set to continue with the next generation, Edward and Maria.

Stanway House, Gloucestershire

The seat of Lord Neidpath

Previous spread: *A view of Stanway taken from the church tower.*

It is a pleasantly undulating journey west from Stow-on-the-Wold towards Tewkesbury. The road runs up and down the hills, with wide open fields at the tops and small villages clustered at the bottoms. After about ten miles this switchbacking comes to an end: quite suddenly the road starts to fall away, bending as it goes, holding on to the side of a steep incline. One last bend and you catch your breath as delightful thatched cottages come into view, their neat front gardens punctuated by small painted gates. Beyond them, the language of the landscape also changes; where you might expect fields of grazing sheep, instead your eye is caught by mighty cedars, copses of specimen trees and, most surprising of all, a large stone pyramid. But as soon as they come into view they are gone, replaced by a leafy tunnel. The trees shelter a crossroads with a fine war memorial: a bronze figure of St George in the process of dispatching the writhing dragon. A small sign hanging nearby heralds Stanway and turning to the right a lane runs down the final slope of the escarpment.

Here you are confronted by one of the architectural masterpieces of the early seventeenth century; an elaborate gatehouse, set between a high wall and the village church. Even the mellow Cotswold stone, the utter charm of the snug cottages, the arching trees and the small gardens cannot temper its extravagant qualities. This is architecture of the utmost sophistication, echoing not so much late-Tudor and Jacobean manor houses but contemporary collegiate buildings in Oxford. In its centre lies a classical porch with doors wide enough to allow horse-drawn carts to pass, a pair of castellated three-storeyed bays stand like sentinels on either side and its roofline is enlivened by shaped gables topped with upright scallop shells

The Gatehouse, built for
Paul Tracy (1550–1625).

— an armorial clue to the owners of the house. The immense wooden doors of
the gatehouse are also decorated, not with armorial shells, but with naturalistic
carvings of rabbits which one suspects were resident here long before the Tracys,
who came here in the middle of the sixteenth century.

It must be nearly thirty years ago that I first came to this sequestered spot at the
very point where the Vale of Evesham meets the Cotswolds, midway between
the prosperous villages of Broadway and Winchcombe. A friend in London was
arranging an exhibition devoted to that late-Victorian political and intellectual
coterie nicknamed The Souls, and she asked if I would call at Stanway to collect
a picture she had arranged to borrow. Here was an opportunity to discover what
lay beyond that gatehouse and the high wall. I still remember pulling into the
rear courtyard to be met with a cluster of ancient cars and, diffidently emerging
from a small door, the young owner. Jamie Neidpath had recently come to live

Anthony Tracy Beck, Esq.
Lady Susan Hamilton, his Wife,
Charlotte Vis.ss Hereford
Susan Lady Elcho, their daughters

Opposite: *Anthony and Susan Tracy-Keck with their daughters Charlotte (later Viscountess Hereford) and Susan (later Lady Elcho) by Henry Alcock circa 1747.*

Left: *Francis Charteris, Lord Elcho (1749–1808), who married Susan Tracy-Keck in 1771, by Archibald Skirving.*

here. His life was hovering between his scholarly pursuits and running the estate. He seemed to live mainly in a large cellar-like kitchen in which plates of food fought for space amidst piles of books and journals. At weekends the house filled with friends, but during the week a black labrador was his principal companion. The rest of the day passed in a pleasant blur of wine and conversation, although not before he had shown me the house.

The house offered a succession of quiet shocks and surprises. A heavy block-oak staircase led from the kitchen to a tiny passage with a large Dutch seventeenth-century picture, *A Party of Boors* by David Ryckaert, hanging over an equally large log box, whilst on the other wall was a case of early nineteenth-century military uniforms. Up a further flight of stairs and into a corridor, we passed gilt eighteenth-century furniture standing beneath beautiful pastel portraits of the *Lord and Lady Elcho* by the Scottish painter Archibald Skirving. In the far room

Mary Wyndham, Lady Elcho, later Countess of Wemyss by Sir Edward Poynter P.R.A. Her waist was only 18 inches.

and hung against a delicious shade of green were paintings of three of The Souls: *Lady Elcho* by Poynter, *The Hon. Percy Wyndham* by Lord Leighton and *Sir Arthur Balfour* by Sargent. Over the fireplace was a family group of the Tracy-Kecks by the itinerant painter Henry Alcock, caught up in a wayward gilt frame.

Retracing our steps, we poked our noses into the small Library with books pouring out of the shelves in piles, obliterating even the grand piano. Jamie then threw open the door to another room, dark save for the shafts of light coming through cracks in the shutters. From the slight echo, you sensed its large scale, but nothing prepared me for what I saw. As the shutters swung back, full-length portraits by Raeburn and Romney emerged out of the dark, clusters of apparently naked women appeared underneath pagodas and a huge Chinese pot sat like a Buddha on a table in the middle of the room. The whole effect was slightly blurred by the paucity of light and a delicate film of ash from the great fireplace. Without a pause, Jamie set off again through a far door and down a precipitous staircase: the house follows the incline of the hill. He led me into a high hall dominated by a spectacular oriel window, beneath which was placed an eighteenth-century exercise chair, presumably so that as you bounced up and down you caught sight of the gardens beyond.

Along one wall stood a huge oak table with a strangely scored top, and along another were fine tapestries and what I thought to be portraits of the Archduke Albrecht and his wife, the Archduchess Isabella, patrons of the young Rubens. The tour ended in a smaller room, an eighteenth-century parlour, its corners housing cabinets of brightly coloured porcelain with botanical designs, its walls hung with family portraits of late-seventeenth-century Tracys. In the corridor that led back to the kitchen, a painting of still life caught my eye. I turned it over and as if to answer my rather blatant curiosity, it was inscribed 'Goddard Dunning made me'. Sadly, I was none the wiser, not knowing who Goddard Dunning was (not, perhaps, surprisingly as this seventeenth-century artist has a recorded output of only three paintings – this makes a fourth). Some hours later I left, with even more questions about the house than when I had arrived. Stanway was not just an unusually splendid Jacobethan manor. Why should such masterpieces of English and Scottish portraiture be sharing a house with Chinese-inspired furniture; why

the William Morris wallpaper and portraits of late-nineteenth-century beauties with wasp waists and flaming red hair; and what was that huge building silhouetted against the church which I noticed for the first time?

The Great Hall with the exercising chair on the right. And beyond the great oriel window.

It is, in fact, that building – a barn built of local limestone with a stone-tiled roof – which gives the clue to the house's existence. It was a huge agricultural store and its unusual position next to the church was no accident. The lands at Stanway had in the early eighth century belonged to two Mercian nobles with the unlikely names of Odo and Dodo, who in 715 gave the property to the abbey of Tewkesbury as its first endowment. The Benedictine abbey grew in power, prestige and wealth under the patronage of a string of Norman families, the FitzHamons, the FitzRoys and the de Clares and during the latter period, circa 1370, this great barn was built. It was used as the storehouse for the tithes (taxes

payable in the form of grain) that were the abbey's economic foundation. The walls are incredibly thick and punctuated only by small slit windows at the gable ends. These let in fresh air and were just wide enough to admit barn owls, whose presence limited the numbers of rats and mice. The roof is supported by massive oak timbers. Base crucks extend from braces in the walls up to the collars, supported by equally massive wind-braces. There are large double doors, intended for carts to enter and unload, but you can also gain access by a smaller side door. Inside, your eyes slowly become accustomed to the lack of light and you become increasingly amazed at the sheer scale of the building. In the silence, intensified by the thickness of the walls, you get a sense of what it must have been like with literally thousands of sacks of grain stacked up at the end of the harvest, with just the noise of a scurrying mouse to disturb the peace. What a contrast to the hurly-burly of wagons arriving, and monks and clerks checking everything with occasional flashes of argument over the weight of grain.

The barn has been carefully maintained and restored by the family over the years. This great storehouse provides a very direct link to monastic England in the Middle Ages. The same can be said of the adjacent pond with its run-in for the horses and carts – not only giving the former a chance to drink but also put moisture back into dried-out wooden wheels, without which the iron hoops around them would come adrift.

Tewkesbury Abbey dominated this area until its suppression in 1530. The abbey buildings were then acquired by the town whose name it bore and the estate of Stanway was leased to Richard Tracy, the younger son of Sir William Tracy from nearby Toddington. The youthful Tracy was an active agent in the Reformation, a protégé of Henry VIII's chief minister, Thomas Cromwell. As well as laying his hands on Stanway, he was instrumental in the dissolution of the great Cistercian abbey of Hailes, which sheltered under the Cotswold escarpment a few miles to the south. That abbey had been founded in 1251 by Richard, Earl of Cornwall and later King of the Romans, the younger son of King John. Some twenty years later it received a phial of the blood of Christ, complete with a guarantee of its authenticity from Pope Urban IV, which made it an important centre of pilgrimage. In 1539 the abbot and twenty monks surrendered the abbey to Tracy, who famously dismissed their holy relic as nothing but 'duck's blood tinted with saffron'.

Richard Tracy's Stanway would have consisted of a cluster of buildings including the abbot's lodgings, described as a 'fair stone house'. What remains of it is embedded in the east wing. The early-Tudor arch to the library passage is probably

a survival from that period, possibly the great plain oak staircase rising to the first floor. It seems likely that Tracy initially occupied these buildings, careful not to overextend himself as he watched the political and religious situation develop. Thomas Cromwell went to the executioner's block and Henry VIII's daughter, Queen Mary, returned the country to Catholicism. But by the late sixteenth century, after the defeat of the Spanish Armada, English Protestantism was more firmly established and the new gentry felt more secure. Richard Tracy's son Paul felt sufficiently confident to extend the house, which he did in spectacular fashion by adding a new wing to the west, complete with Great Hall, offices and kitchens. His hall remains, still lit by its great oriel window with over 700 separate panes of glass – a testimony to the family's architectural aspirations and acquired wealth. Here the household's communal meals would have been taken, the family seated on a raised dias and everyone else in the body of the room, called the 'marsh' because it was low-lying. Whilst the original dining table has gone, another that dates from just a few decades later survives, possibly on account of its weight and length that would make it almost impossible to remove. This is no ordinary table, either, but a shuffleboard, standing along the west wall with its decorated side facing into the room and its plain back towards the wall. It must date from around 1620 and would have been commissioned by either Sir Paul Tracy, 1st Bt. (he was made a baronet by James I in 1611) or his son, Sir Richard Tracy, 2nd Bt. The massive table top is made from a single piece of oak. At one end it is scored with a starting line from which you send brass counters sliding down to the far end, praying that they do not fly off the highly polished surface in the process. For the counters to score, they must come to rest between a series of lines at the far end, a successful 'shuffle' being rewarded with either one or two points. Players' scores have been recorded for the past hundred years and the highest remains at 15. This score has been achieved on just three occasions, the most recent being on 6 September 1950 by Jamie's grandmother. Jamie's personal best was registered on 9 January 1959, when he was 10. Early-seventeenth-century shuffleboard tables are extremely rare – in fact only three seem to have survived in good order complete with their counters. Nearby is an early-eighteenth-century painting by Balthazar Nebot showing one such table in use outside an inn. A wedding gift to the present Lord Neidpath from his father, the Earl of Wemyss.

An interest in the past and respect for earlier owners' achievements characterizes many developments at Stanway, especially in the nineteenth and twentieth centuries. This is certainly true of the Jacobean-style ceiling that was replaced in 1860, and the arrangements of the hangings and tapestries that date from 1949. Indeed, the general harmony is so persuasive that it takes a little time to realize that the screen at the far end of the room cannot possibly be part of the original architectural language. Indeed, it speaks of the Palladian classicism of the early eighteenth century. It was almost certainly designed by Francis Smith, whose name appears in the family accounts, and like his buildings in his native Warwick and the surrounding country houses, it employs the full classical

Opposite: The Great Hall showing the shuffleboard with decorated side facing the room, dated circa 1620 and the classical screen at the far end of the room, probably designed by Francis Smith of Warwick.

Right: *Coloured engraving taken from Sir Robert Atkins' The Ancient and Present State of Gloucestershire, showing Stanway in the early 18th century.*

Opposite: *The mid 17th-century West Front with doorcase added by John Tracy (1681–1735).*

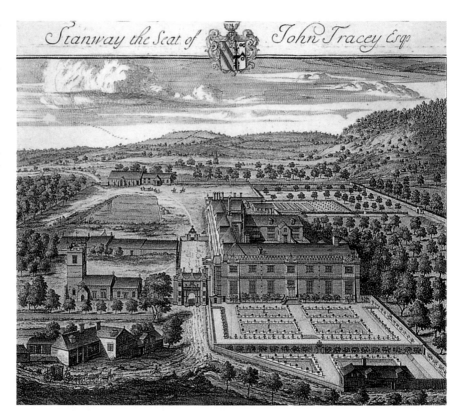

repertory of columns, capitals and architraves. Behind the screen is a panelled wall of the same period, punctuated by a Tudor-style door, probably inserted in the nineteenth century. These juxtapositions are now tempered by the passage of time, but they reveal the ebb and flow of architectural change that has taken place since the sixteenth century.

The economic basis for the estate is made very clear in an adjacent room aptly named the Audit Room. It is here that over the centuries tenants have come to pay their quarterly rents in person. The estate, now some 5,000 acres, is entirely let to tenants and these occasions give them (and their landlord) an opportunity to discuss problems and identify solutions. The original rent table still stands here, a wonder of craftsmanship and technology dating from the late eighteenth century. On a square base, the circular leather-lined mahogany top can revolve to reveal a succession of drawers in the frieze, each inscribed with letters of the alphabet. The original rent books would have been stored here. The table would have been swung round to reveal the relevant letter, the drawer unlocked, the rent agreed and marked up, the book safely returned and the money placed in a fitted well in the very centre of the table, with a special compartment for notes and a secret catch to prevent theft.

The estate grew rich enough during the early seventeenth century to allow Sir Richard's son, Sir Humphrey Tracy, 3rd Bt., to significantly extend the house that he inherited in 1637. He rebuilt the central block on the south side, between

his grandfather's Great Hall and what remained of the original abbot's lodging. Here he created a single large room, the Great Parlour (now the Drawing Room) with a central fireplace and a succession of windows along the garden front. This handsome space reflects not only the changing use of rooms at that time but also the desire to provide family areas on a larger scale. Its regularity and noble proportions still come as a surprise. If Sir Humphrey had further plans to bring the house up to date, these were lost in the maelstrom of the Civil War. He sided with the king, and was later obliged to pay Parliament some £1,600 in order to retain his estate. It is now somewhat ironic that Edward Pierce's sensitive marble bust of Oliver Cromwell should preside over the passage that leads from the Hall to Sir Humphrey's Great Parlour. Sir Humphrey died in 1651 and was succeeded by his two brothers in turn, neither of whom had descendants. Thus in 1677, on the death of the last sibling, the ownership of the estate leapt across to their distant cousin, Ferdinando Tracy, the son of Viscount Tracy of Toddington, and five years later to his son, John.

John Tracy (d.1735) was related through his mother, Katherine, to the Keck family of Great Tew in Oxfordshire, and through his wife, Anne, to the Atkyns

family of Sapperton in south Gloucestershire. In due course the former connection was to bring additional land to the estate. The latter connected him not only to one of the leading English judicial families, but also to Sir Robert Atkyns, author of *The Ancient and Present State of Gloucestershire* published in 1712. Sir Robert Atkyns may well have encouraged the improvements brought about by John and Anne Tracy. The house was provided with fashionable sash windows and the gatehouse given a fine new pedimented central section, replete with the couple's armorial achievements. Similarly, a classical doorcase was added to the south front, again with the Tracy arms impaling those of Atkyns.

Externally, the landscape was transformed. Taking full advantage of the house's rather unusual position, banked up against the steeply rising ground, a terrace was created which fed out to avenues of newly planted trees running north and south. This terrace was wide enough to accommodate that most fashionable of water features, a canal – large enough for the family to ply a boat or go fishing. To feed the canal, water was diverted from springs high up on the escarpment, and the powerful flow down the steep incline enabled the creation of a water staircase. A gentle tinkling sound was created as the water descended the carefully constructed falls, the different heights and lengths creating a variety of notes. A local artist, William Taylor of Worcester, was given the task of capturing these changes, and his charming, somewhat naive view, still hangs at Stanway. The artist's first problem was the near impossible task of incorporating the water cascade with its canal. If he were simply to stand at the top and paint what he saw, the cascade would disappear in a few foreshortened inches. Yet if he stood at the bottom, the wide canal would simply appear as a narrow strip.

The Stanway Pyramid, erected by Robert Tracy, circa 1750, possibly to the design of Thomas Wright.

Taylor managed brilliantly (if not accurately) to include everything through the simple trick of turning the cascade through ninety degrees. His straightforward approach is what gives the painting its extraordinary charm. The house with the church beyond are shown to the left of the canvas. Behind lies the estate, with clusters of trees demarcating the fields in which cattle graze. On the terraced lawns the family are shown with friends, enjoying the day – some playing games, others walking and a further group aboard a boat on the canal.

By the time Taylor painted the house and garden, John Tracy had died and been succeeded by his eldest son, Robert. He must have commissioned the painting to commemorate his father's achievements, and this was not his only act of filial piety. Robert was also responsible for the strangest object in this Gloucester landscape – the Stanway Pyramid. Built of local honey-coloured stone, and now surrounded by great trees, the pyramid has almost taken its place in the land-scape yet still has the capacity to shock. Pyramids were adopted by the Romans as a suitable design for mausoleums, and they entered English consciousness in the late-sixteenth century, although it was not until the early eighteenth that the first monumental pyramid was erected by Hawksmoor as part of his fantastic fortifications surrounding Castle Howard in Yorkshire. There the pyramid tops a gateway; at Stanway, even more spectacularly, it sits on an open grassy knoll on top of the hill. You cannot help but be impressed by the precision of its design and the sharp interplay between the four decorative urns to each corner and the mathematical severity of its shape. Standing beneath it and looking up into its cavity, it is the exactness of the cut stone that takes your breath away. You are almost grateful that the elaborate plaster ceiling was removed in 1945 to reveal this awe-inspiring space. On its west side, fronting the cascade, is a stone tablet lettered in Latin, which translates to read: 'To the happy memory of John Tracy, Gentleman, a man who, although easily distinguished by his ancient lineage, was yet by his own virtues even more distinguished than his race. Robert Tracy, Gentleman, his son has therefore in piety caused this building, such as it is, to be erected in the year of mankind's salvation 1750'.

In the eighteenth century the landscape could be viewed not only from the hill-side but also from the top of the house itself, where a parapet walk ran around the roof. This has recently been restored by Jamie Neidpath and once again you can look down on the house and out across the gardens into the estate. Clambering up through the attics, you travel along the edge of the roof protected by a parapet built of the same beautiful local oolitic limestone, taken from some of the thirty-two quarries to be found on the estate. Over the years different coloured lichens have grown there, their colours, ranging from deep ochre to a sharp black, enriching its surface. On one side of the parapet walk you look across to the roofline of the gatehouse topped by its upright scallop shells. In the other direction, across the canal, lies the large walled kitchen garden. In midsummer the currant bushes under their nets dangle with black, red and translucent white fruit, recalling the decoration that appears on a number of Chelsea porcelain plates in the cabinet in the Audit Room. From the 1750s the Chelsea artists had access to botanical drawings owned by Sir Hans Sloane, apothecary, antiquarian and supervisor of the Chelsea Physic Garden. These provided ideas for decorating their new wares in an entirely original way, making the most of interweaving plants and their fruits with insects and bugs.

In the mid eighteenth century, at the time the Chelsea plates were coming out of the kiln, family life at Stanway began to falter. Although Robert Tracy was one of a dozen children, neither he nor his brothers had male heirs and so in 1773 the estate passed to his eldest niece, Henrietta. The following year she married Edward Devereux, 12th Viscount Hereford, Premier Viscount of England. She moved away, but returned to Stanway a decade later following her husband's early death, and lived out a long widowhood there with her dogs as companions until 1810. The estate then passed to the eldest son of her younger sister Susan, who had married Francis Charteris, Lord Elcho, in 1771.

Lord Elcho's portrait by Edinburgh's leading portraitist, Sir Henry Raeburn, hangs in the Drawing Room. Raeburn produced a wonderfully commanding full-length image of this Scottish nobleman, intentionally limiting his palette of colours to a range of dark greens, browns and dark greys. It is in striking contrast to George Romney's pair of group portraits showing his wife Susan and their children, with their relaxed compositions and use of lighter colours. He painted these charming pictures in 1780, charging the not inconsiderable sum then of 70 guineas apiece – perhaps taking into account the truism that children are not often the easiest of sitters! Maybe the young boy holding the strings of his kite helped to control his siblings – this is the Hon. Francis Charteris, aged eight at

that time, who would inherit Stanway from his aunt Henrietta, Lady Hereford, in 1817. By that time, he had also inherited his family's title and become the 8th Earl of Wemyss, together with their great estates in Scotland centred on Gosford, east of Edinburgh along the Firth of Forth, and Amisfield near Haddington.

It was for Amisfield that the pair of exotic day beds, standing in the middle of the Drawing Room at Stanway, were made around 1760. These are a real flight of fantasy; sofas designed to look like Chinese pavilions. The hipped roofs rise to open loggias enlivened by chinoiserie ornaments, including a company of small hanging bells that move when you shift position on the couch below. Along the edges runs painted Chinese fretwork, reflected on the surface of the fine carved mahogany post that holds the whole confection aloft. Yet the only element that is genuinely Chinese is the hand-painted wallpaper that lines the underside of the roof. As you recline, you look up at an extraordinarily colourful world of flowers and birds evoking far-off exotic lands. The master craftsman Thomas Chippendale designed these sofas, and published them in his *Gentlemen and Cabinet Maker's Directory* in 1754. Many of his more fantastic ideas were never realized, and the same fate might well have befallen these day beds but for a sole patron, Mr Francis Charteris, who decided that they were just what he needed for his new house in East Lothian. Two hundred and fifty years later they still astound visitors when they enter his descendant's Drawing Room in Gloucestershire.

Opposite: *The Drawing Room showing the pagoda daybeds designed by Thomas Chippendale with the portrait of Lord Elcho by Sir Henry Raeburn beyond. A painting of his children, by George Romney, hangs above the fireplace.*

Above: *One of the pair of pictures by Louis-Jean-François Lagrenée the Elder, Les Grâces Lutinées Par Les Amours, in the Drawing Room.*

The stunning paintings by the French court painter Lagrenée, which hang behind Chippendale's day bed, also came from Scotland. The Three Graces (Aglaia, Thalia and Euphrosyne), the classical bestowers of beauty and charm, sprawl languorously across another day bed, each lightly clad. All would be peaceful were it not for the annoying amorini, depicted as pesky children, whom the Graces have had to reprimand, one brandishing a whip. These sensuous paintings were first seen at the Salon in Paris in 1770. They evoke the world of François Boucher and Henry Fragonard, but with a new awareness of classical detail and an absence of the frothy use of paint that characterized the rococo period. These are the largest and most accomplished works by this artist in Britain, looking just as fresh as when newly arrived from Paris.

In some ways the paintings in the Drawing Room reflect life at Stanway today. The seriousness of the Raeburn portrait has resonance in the intelligent running of the estate by the current Lord Neidpath, and the work for the Beckley Foundation overseen by his wife, Amanda. The foundation, which takes its name from her family home near Oxford, researches consciousness and its altered states, advising politicians on the effects of drug dependency. Family life, evoked by the Romneys, is still at the heart of the house with Jamie and Amanda's children. Last, and certainly not least, the house parties that they love to hold echo the gaiety expressed in the Lagrenée scenes.

Such a balance of serious thought and fun was the very essence of life for the small coterie of friends who gathered here at the end of the nineteenth century. They were invited by Hugo, Lord Elcho (later 11th Earl of Wemyss) and his wife, Mary Wyndham. The cerebral nature of their entertainment distinguished them from many of their contemporaries, and gave rise to the nickname The Souls. Stanway provided an ideal weekend retreat for them, close enough to be reached from London by rail on Saturday mornings and to return from the following Monday. It was here that the young Arthur Balfour (later prime minister), the equally youthful George Curzon (later viceroy of India) and a host of young Tennants, Manners and Wyndhams would find time to talk and play. Their games included not just croquet and tennis, but others of their own invention, such as Margot Tennant's 'Obituaries' – Arthur Balfour was understandably rather shocked to come across one written rather mischievously by her, opening with the words 'So Arthur Balfour is dead!' The Stanway life of The Souls is captured in an album of sepia photographs. There are also paintings by their favoured artists; Sir Edward Poynter, Sir Edward Burne-Jones, George Frederick Watts, Lady Violet Lindsay (the Duchess of Rutland) and John Singer Sargent. Many of these are gathered in the Boudoir at the far end of the house, where Amanda Neidpath often works. This room has a wonderfully calm atmosphere; one can almost hear the gentle rhythm of late-night conversation before The Souls turned in for the night, their bedrooms appropriately wallpapered with designs by William Morris, left untouched since that time. Another survivor is a stamp stuck to the ceiling of the Great Hall. In the late 1920s there were twenty up there, flicked into place by

a spinning coin sent skywards by James Barry (of *Peter Pan* fame) or one of his guests. He took Stanway for the summer months, inviting friends to stay and join in games of cricket and tennis, or amateur theatricals in the great barn.

The Boudoir at the end of the house with a window looking up to the terrace.

For the family the aftermath of the Great War was a sad time. Lord Wemyss's heir, Ego, Lord Elcho, had been killed during active service in 1916 and his widow, Lady Violet Manners, was left to bring up their two infant sons, David (now 12th Earl of Wemyss and father of Jamie) and Martin (who would become Lord Charteris, Provost of Eton). It was on his grandmother's death that Jamie came to live at Stanway. Over the past thirty years, he and Amanda have revived the special qualities of this place, and built on the achievements of his ancestors. In addition to restoring the cascade and canal, they have added a waterspout, the highest hydraulically fed example in Europe, which now bursts out of the centre of the calm waters. As it rises a spectacular 300 feet into the air, it is another tantalizing feature of the landscape that travellers may notice as they make their way down the winding Stanway Hill.

Acknowledgements

The series and this book would not have been possible without the kindness, support and energy of the owners of the houses and their staff. I would like to extend my wholehearted thanks to:

John and Gina Berkeley and their sons, Charles and Henry; Edmund and Marion Brudenell and their daughter, Anna Maria, who worked with me at Sotheby's and introduced me to her parents; Hugh and Grania Cavendish and their punk aardvark; Philip and Isobel De L'Isle, who were brave enough to be filmed first; Simon and Victoria Leatham, and Jon Culverhouse, the curator at Burghley, with best wishes for a stimulating future; Charles and Caroline Legard and the ever-smiling gardeners at Scampston; Jamie and Amanda Neidpath and the engineer behind their water shute; Eddie and Georgina Norfolk, their polymath librarian John Martin Robinson and all the staff at Arundel; the Duke of Richmond and his son, Charles March, who, together with Rosemary Baird, made our time at Goodwood so exhilarating; Neil and Deirdre Rosebery, whose enthusiastic response from the outset of the project was a real tonic; John and Jo Wingfield-Digby, the next generation, Edward and Maria and the family's grape-guzzling Labrador. Indeed, a special thanks must go to all the dogs that took part, showing a delightfully critical aptitude – walking away when I talked too much!

This also gives me an opportunity to all those involved in making the series, the principal producer, Joanna Bartholomew, together with Charles Cooper and the late John Williams. My thanks also go to the film crew, Peter Eason and Paul Cox; I am and will always be in your debt. And, of course, Denys Blakeway and all the team at his eponymous company, particularly Elizabeth Jones and Kate Macky who have kept me on course.

This book was the brainchild of Kim Peat at Channel Five, and her vision has been made real by Richard Milner, Bruno Vincent and their colleagues at Pan Macmillan.

Supporting me at the office has been Sandra Orme, a tower of strength and full of sensible suggestions and, at home, my wife Mary.

Postscript

It would have been invidious to have written about houses that you cannot explore for yourself. I have chosen houses that are open to the public on a regular basis. To find out more about their opening times, please refer to the following web sites:

1 www.arundelcastle.org
2 www.berkeley-castle.com
3 www.burghley.co.uk
4 www.dalmeny.co.uk
5 www.deenepark.com
6 www.goodwood.co.uk
7 www.holker-hall.co.uk
8 www.penshurstplace.co.uk
9 www.scampston.co.uk
10 www.sherbornecastle.com
11 www.stanwayfountain.co.uk

I hope you will enjoy seeing these houses and their collections at first hand. It is a world of infinite variety, but be warned, I have discovered that the more you think you know about them, the more you realize how much there is left to explore.

Picture Credits

All pictures reproduced with the kind permission of the owners of the respective houses, with the exception of:

Dalmeny

The Beauvais Tapestry p.95, Archibald, 5th Earl of Rosebery by Millais p.89, Edward Gibbon by Reynolds p.88, Mentmore by Brewer p.90, gaming machine by Gallonde p.97, The Napoleon Room p.94
© Antonia Reeve Photography

Goodwood

Egyptian Dining Room p.141 by Christopher Simon Sykes, House & Garden © The Condé Nast Publications Ltd
The Card Room p.137, Sèvres wine cooler p.136, The Ballroom pp.126–7
© Stephen Hayward
Goodwood Revival p.142 © John Colley
Tapestry Drawing Room p.138 © Mike Caldwell

Holker Hall

Entrance porch p.148, exterior of Holker from the Gardens pp.144–5
© Julie C. Chambers
The Hall p.150, The Library p.153 and the Duke's Bedroom p.165
© Jarrold Publishing/Holker Hall, reproduced by kind permission of the publisher

Scampston Hall

Scampston Hall by Marlow p.194, William Thomas Darby St Quintin by Opie p.202, The South Library p.204, Scampston exterior pp.188-9
© Tim Imrie/Country Life Picture Library
View of Bath by Garvey p.196, Sir William St Quintin by Kneller p.192, French commode p.205, pair of Sèvres candlesticks p.209, The Venus Marina p.208, Lady Legard by Wright of Derby p.206, Cypron and her brood by Gilpin p.195, Sir Digby Legard by Batoni p.207, Wooded landscape by Gainsborough p.197 © Richard Clive
Bridge Building by 'Capability' Brown drawn by Francis Nicholson p.198
© Richard Holttum
Sir William St Quintin by Gainsborough p.191 © Stephen Brayne

Every effort has been made by the publishers to contact the copyright holders of the images used in this book. If in any case the correct copyright line has not been used the publishers will ensure that this is rectified in all future editions.